Culture Defeats Strategy

7 Lessons on Leadership from a Texas High School Football Coach

**Randy Jackson
Head Football Coach
Grapevine High School
Grapevine, Texas**

WHAT CHAMPIONS ARE SAYING ABOUT RANDY JACKSON AND *CULTURE DEFEATS STRATEGY*:

"I have known Randy for many years and consider him to be one of the best High School Coaches in Texas. His ability to motivate and share his vision to his coaches and players is what sets him apart. This book will give you insight into how he defines his Culture both in his program and in life. I am inspired every time I get to visit with Randy. This book is a must read for anyone looking to bring out the best in themselves and their team."

Chad Morris
Head Football Coach
Southern Methodist University

Coach: Do you want to win more? Here are two things you can do right now –

#1. Go to Grapevine, Texas and spend a season on Coach Randy Jackson's staff.
or . . .
#2. Read Coach Jackson's remarkable book, "Culture Defeats Strategy."

This book will change you, it will improve your program and it'll help you WIN MORE. I guarantee it! I don't care what sport you coach, you'll find a ton of incredibly simple, but amazingly powerful techniques and strategies that'll be instantly effective!"

Dr. Rob Gilbert
Professor of Applied Sport Psychology
Montclair State University (NJ)
Founder of Success Hotline

I hired Randy right out of Northeast Louisiana University in 1990 for his first coaching job. Immediately I recognized his talented mind and exuberance for innovative ideas. "Culture defeats Strategy" is a must read for all coaches because it provides innovative ideas and sound philosophy that will ensure improvement in any athletic program. Randy and I have been close friends and collaborators for over two decades and he has shared many of his ideas with me over the years. I am glad that he has taken the time to share these ideas, philosophies, and innovations with you. Randy Jackson is a WINNER and so is this book!

Phil Blue
Executive Director of Athletics
Abilene I.S.D.

I have known Randy Jackson since his days at Lone Oak High School and he was a frequent visitor to Wylie High School where I was the head football coach and athletic director. I was impressed with him then and my respect for him has only increased since. Coach Jackson's character, integrity, passion, and tenacity ooze from this book. I would encourage any athletic director to read and share this book with all of his or her head coaches. The reader will find at least one thing in this book that will strike a chord with his or her program. If you want to build a program or take your program to the next level this is a must read.

Mark Ball
Retired Head Football Coach and
Athletic Director in Texas

Coach Randy Jackson has scored a touchdown with this book! I've coached football for 15 years here in Southern California, and could not stop reading it tonight! Jackson has woven together some dynamite stories and real life lessons from a lifetime coaching at every level in Texas to keep the reader interested and challenged. Not only football coaches will garner applicable principles. From the "5 Minute Rule" to "Winning The National Anthem" to practical team building strategies, this book has a little bit of it all. As an Athletic Director, when I give my coaches something to read, I tell them to "just pick out one thing, apply that this season and grow." With this book, you can easily pick out 10 new ideas to apply to your program!"

Chris Fore - Eight Laces Consulting
Southern California

Coach Jackson is a master of the mental game and expert at intentionally building culture. Many programs have a great culture but I've found much of the time they are hard to reproduce. Coach Jackson provides specific and reproducible methods for how you can intentionally build a championship culture in your program.

Nathan Stanley
Athletic Director / Head Football Coach
Redmond High School, Redmond, Oregon

Culture Defeats Strategy

7 Lessons on Leadership From a Texas High School Football Coach

©2016 by Randy A. Jackson

Printed in the United States of America

Edited by: Cliff Gibson

Randy Jackson
Culture Defeats Strategy
7 Lessons on Leadership From a Texas High School Football
Coach

ISBN-13: 978-1534696549

ISBN-10: 1534696547

If this book has a positive impact on the way you coach or lead your program please email me. I would love to hear about it and develop a relationship with a like-minded coach.

My website is: CoachRandyJackson.com

You can also reach me on Twitter **@CoachJacksonTPW**.

I also speak at clinics and would love the opportunity to do this if you are in need of a speaker on creating culture, leadership or football.

Thanks so much for reading this book.

I hope it becomes one of your 'go-to' books on creating culture and leadership.

Randy Jackson

CONTENTS

DEDICATION

This book is dedicated to my family. My wife, Shannon, who has followed me all over Texas allowing me to chase my dreams of leading high school football teams and athletic departments. We have been married 21 years and she has been my rock. She has been there on the field after the biggest wins, hugged me after our biggest losses and stood in front of a school board and told them how wrong they were when I was reassigned in a little east Texas town. We have lived in 14 houses during our time together and she has made each one a home. Knowing each time it was not a permanent place.

To my son Russ and my daughter Katie. Like all coaches' kids they don't see me enough. You both make me more proud than you know. I love you all.

My dad, Raymond, was also a coach. He led teams for 41 years in Texas. The last 22 in the small community of Tenaha near the Louisiana border. He was the head football and basketball coach for the last 17 years of his career.

What a tremendous advantage to grow up in the same house with a successful coach. To say my father taught me a lot would be an understatement. On December 22, 2015 he passed away after a long battle with cancer. I miss being able to pick up the phone and call him after a big win or a tough loss. He was special, patient and cared about people. He was a character who always had a story that you weren't really sure if it was true or not; it usually was. He was that type of guy. My dad always encouraged me and I knew he was proud I became a coach. My only regret on writing this book is I didn't do it soon enough for him to read it. He would have been proud like always.

ACKNOWLEDGMENTS

It is with sincere and deep appreciation that I, Randy Jackson, acknowledge the support and guidance of the following people who helped make this book possible:

Special thanks to Brian Cain, Dr. Rob Gilbert, Jay Zeller, and Matt Morse for your guidance and help with my first book. Thanks to Cliff Gibson for editing. I know this was a big task!

Thanks to the hundreds of high school and college coaches who have shared their strategies with me on culture, toughness and leadership and have influenced the writing of this book.

Thanks, Phil Blue, for giving me my first coaching job back in 1990, but more importantly for mentoring me ever since. Thanks for always answering my phone calls and taking the time to be a friend of wisdom, advice and guidance.

All the players I have had the honor to coach. Thank you from the bottom of my heart. At times I have been impatient, too critical and downright wrong. Thanks for giving me 100% anyway. I love coaching and it has been a true honor to coach all of you.

Thanks to all the coaches and administrators I have worked with over the years. Thank you for putting up with me. Thank you for all your efforts and hours we spent trying to make men of character and win games along the way.

All the parents who have tirelessly worked in the booster clubs over the years and helped make each stop a little more special for each player. Thank you Grapevine parents, you are part of the turnaround and it is going to keep getting better!

FOREWORD

Culture and leadership development is the difference between good and great programs. Coach Jackson is one of the nation's best at both. Having worked in the field of Peak Performance, leadership and championship culture education, I travel all over the country working with coaches in all sports at all levels. Coach Jackson is a true innovator and at the forefront of coaching the mental game and his program at is a first-rate example of how a championship culture can and should be created.

I met Coach Jackson during an athletic staff development for Grapevine-Colleyville ISD in Texas. Shortly after, I began working with him 1-1 to help him grow as a coach as he was looking for an edge and to become the best version of him that he had ever been. I think I have learned from him and benefited from our relationship as much as I have with anyone I have ever worked with.

Coach Jackson is a man on a mission. Not only did he implement strategies we discussed, but he also attacked them with passion. We discussed what leaders should look like and how they need to model the physical fitness attributes that they want in their athletes. People need a model to see and a motto to say. Coach Jackson began exercising and following a nutrition plan and was committed to losing 30lbs and getting into the best shape of his life. He did it. I mentioned the Success Hotline and how calling this as part of my routine had been life chancing and he not only calls it every day, but also uses it with his team and has developed a relationship with Dr. Rob Gilbert the creator of success hotline. We talked about core principles as the foundation of a leadership program and his program is now as strong an example of this as there is in sport.

This past season I encouraged him to write a book. In true Coach Jackson form he said, "I'm in" and knocked it out of the park. I have even had Coach Jackson speak at mental game trainings for my clients and he is always one of the most popular parts of the program.

This book is an in-depth look at what coaching for character in sport is all about. And you get to experience it at the highest level in Texas High School Football. Coach Jackson uses his experiences and story-telling ability to provide a system and process that will allow you to connect with your players on a deeper level, create a championship culture and provide a foundation for accelerated player development. He lays out his culture building strategies in an easy to read and understandable format. Any coach in any sport will benefit from the many ideas, strategies and the wisdom he shares from his 26 years in the trenches as a high school coach.

Peak performance is a lifestyle, not an event, and the principles shared in this book will not only help you as a coach maximize your *team's* potential, it will help you maximize your *life* potential. Better coaches make better athletic programs, and better athletic programs produce better players and win more games. What you will learn in this book will be a huge part of future success.

Coach Jackson was successful before our relationship began. I am proud to see how he continues to grow and have a tremendously positive impact on the people who call him Coach. He was named the Tom Landry Coach of the Year in 2015 and I can't wait to see what the future holds for the programs under his leadership. Using this book to help you take your program go to the next level.

Proud of you, Randy! Keep Dominating the Day!

Brian Cain
Peak Performance Coach
BrianCain.com

AUTHOR'S NOTE

"Coach, why do you want to write a book?" Collin Margiotta, a senior linebacker, asked this question to me during a leadership council meeting. I was telling the guys about my project and wanted them to help hold me accountable. I thought for a second and replied, "Coaching is the most honorable profession in the world when done the right way and I want to do my part to contribute."

I have thought about writing a book for years. One of my first bosses always said, "we should all write a book when we are done". He was talking about the adventures and struggles of being a high school coach. I have enough stories for a book like that also, but this book is about culture and leadership.

I wrote an article for Texas Coach Magazine recently with the same title as this book. A few coaches told me it helped them with their program so the more I thought about it the more motivated I became to take the next step and write this book. My intent for this book is to give coaches of all sports an outline of what culture and leadership is in our program at Grapevine and how to create both for their program.

I believe culture and leadership development is where weight training was thirty years ago. In the 70's and 80's it was much easier to gain an edge over opponents with a great strength and conditioning program. Now, most all programs understand the value of strength development and do a great job with it. The mental game is the next frontier. This is where we can get the edge today.

I am honored to share my thoughts on culture and leadership. I am hopeful you will get a few specific ideas to help your athletes and program overachieve.

CHAPTER 1

TOUGH PEOPLE WIN

> **"Toughness is the product of struggle."**

"Coach, you need to go to the school board meeting tonight. They're going to be talking about you and it isn't good."

My morning ritual was to get coffee at the Texaco station and visit a little while with the retired guys in the community who congregated there. They were a great bunch of men who loved the DeKalb Bears and had a good story or two to tell.

What? That couldn't be. This was April and I had only been in DeKalb, Texas one season, but it was a good season. We were 9-4, district champions and had advanced farther than they had been in the playoffs in 26 years. I had also had my contract renewed two months prior by the board on a 7-0 vote.

I replied, "I'll go, but I'm sure they aren't talking about me."

I went to the board meeting and it was like any other meeting. They went through the normal parts of their agenda and around 8 p.m. they went into executive session to discuss personnel; also standard procedure. To be safe, I decided to stick around for a while.

Around 11 p.m. I was too tired to sit around any longer so I went home. When I went to bed that night I still wasn't thinking much about it. I was sure they were happy with me. If they weren't and wanted to speak with me they knew I was sitting out in the audience at the meeting. It must have been a bad rumor, common in small country towns.

The next morning the Superintendent of schools for DeKalb ISD called me into his office. This is when my life and my families' lives changed.

"Coach, the board met last night and they decided to make a change. You are no longer our athletic director or head football coach. You have a contract for next year with DISD of course, but it won't be as the AD or head football coach.

"You have two options; stay here and be a regular classroom teacher, or resign. I will need to know your decision by Friday."

Thinking back on this still makes me queasy. I asked him what caused this decision by the board. His response was, "They would like the program to go in a different direction." To which I responded, "I don't know what my response will be when we meet again Friday, but I can tell you I won't be resigning."

This was the lowest point in my career. Shannon and I had moved our young family halfway across Texas and planned on staying for several years.

My career was off to a good start, I had led programs for

four seasons at three different schools and had won playoff games at each one. I was 'on my way' in the head coaching profession. There was no way this could be happening.

But things were about to get worse.

I met with the superintendent again on Friday to tell him I would be staying. He wasn't overjoyed by this, as I'm sure he was hoping I would just go away quietly. For the next several days I struggled to get a handle of what I should do next. Like an idiot, I was not a member of a teacher or coach's professional organization that provided free legal counsel.

Any coach reading this should join a professional educator association that provides legal assistance ASAP. In our profession, you never know when you will need an attorney to represent you. I was not going away quietly so I hired counsel to make sure I would know my rights during the process. Not cheap, but it was worth every penny.

Ten days later, I was back in with the superintendent. He hadn't received any reference calls and asked me if I was looking for a job. I said yes, but I wanted to continue to be a head coach and it is tough to find something late in the spring especially, when you have been relieved of your role as athletic director and head football coach.

He said, "The school board wants you to be doing something so I need you to report to ISS on Monday." ISS is 'In School Suspension' for the students who have 'done wrong' so to speak. My attorney told me to make sure I didn't do anything insubordinate, so on Monday morning at 8 a.m. I knocked on the door.

"I'm Coach Jackson. I was told to report here this morning," I told the ISS teacher. I walked into the room and looked around. There was only one teacher's desk. We both realized it at about the same time. "I don't know coach, I guess just sit where you want to."

There were five students in ISS that day. All of them sat in individual cubicles with partitions between seats to keep them from being able to see each other. My only choice was to sit with them, so I did. If you ever want to be humbled, go do some 'hard time' at your local high school's 'In School Suspension' for a few days.

This was 2003 and if there were smartphones I didn't have one. I wasn't prepared to occupy my time so I sat there ... and sat there ... and sat there. Finally, around 11:30 the teacher says, "Lunch." I wasn't sure what to do so I looked at the students for direction. They all got up so I did as well; they all pushed their chairs in so I pushed my chair in. They started walking in a single file line towards the door. I found a gap in the line and got in. I didn't stay in the line all the way to the cafeteria, but you get the point. I was getting punished for not resigning and moving on.

This is a story I was too embarrassed to tell for years. It wasn't something I brought up or felt the need to share, but now I know it is part of my testimony. If you saw this in a movie you would say 'no way, this would never happen.' There is no way a school district would put their athletic director in ISS and sit with the regular students...no way.

God has always protected me and He did with this situation also. I 'escaped' eventually and was able to get my career as a head coach going again. In fact, eight years later I was the 4A Coach of the Year for the state of Texas.

One of the core values I'll discuss in Chapter 5 is toughness. All of us are going through something. If you aren't going through a struggle now, you will be soon. When I started having success on a bigger stage my 'ISS' story became the way I opened my lectures. I figure if they don't really care for my culture or offensive talk they will have heard a really funny story at the beginning.

I stayed in ISS for a few weeks; until school was out in late May. I read a few books. I tried a crossword puzzle each day ... almost finished one.

My contract as athletic director was 228 days, so I reported all summer to my office, which a few weeks after my reassignment had been moved out of the field house and into the gym. I have a few more stories from my time at DeKalb, but those are for another book. In August they got tired of me being there and paid me to leave.

There is not a great book or movie where things are good for the main character the whole time, that would be boring. Struggle and overcoming adversity makes the story interesting and worth reading. Like it usually happens; what happened in DeKalb was turned to good.

Everyone can relate to having to deal with tremendous adversity and having to overcome. It is also an awesome example of how God showed His power by allowing me to move forward afterwards and even prosper beyond my wildest dreams.

> **"Without a struggle there can be no progress."**
>
> **Frederick Douglas**
> **Social Reformer – 1800's**

In this book, I am going to discuss specific strategies that have helped me lead high school football teams in Texas, from the smallest classifications to the largest. I'll discuss the lessons I have learned to build culture and leadership, lessons for you as you advance in your career. I'll also give you specific leadership and culture-building strategies we use for our team in Grapevine, Texas to overachieve. Strategies if you will implement will help your program be successful.

I have been blessed. I grew up in Tenaha, Texas and played every sport that was offered. My father was my head football, basketball and track coach. We had good athletes and won a lot in everything we did. This is where my love of sport was fostered and I am so grateful for the memories I have being coached by my dad. He gave me an up close view of leadership and coaching.

I wasn't a great football player. I was good enough to earn a scholarship to Northeast Louisiana (now Louisiana Monroe), but was never a starter. Growing up in a small town I didn't have to outwork anyone to get playing time and I didn't understand how much effort it took to be a starter at the small Division 1 level.

Playing college football for Pat Collins and being a member of the 1987 1-AA National Champions was one of the greatest things that happened to me. I was in a culture laboratory without ever realizing it. I learned discipline and what intense practices were all about. When my playing career was over I was driven to make my mark in football through coaching. Just being in the program and getting coached by some great leaders like legendary offensive line coach J.B. Grimes, gave me the confidence that I could help make a difference.

GREAT PROGRAMS HAVE GREAT SUPPORT FROM THE ADMINISTRATION. YOUR FIRST JOB IS IMPORTANT. YOU MUST HAVE SUPPORT TO CREATE YOUR CULTURE. MAKE SURE THE ORGANIZATION WILL DO WHAT IT TAKES TO WIN.

I have always been ambitious and a fixer. I love the challenge of building a program. I have moved my beautiful family too many times, but we have met lots of great people on our journey. One of the reasons I feel qualified to write this book is because I have taken over at several schools as the head coach / athletic director and have learned that while all are different, the formula doesn't change much no matter where or what size the school is. A great leader comes in with a vision, provides hope, solves problems and most importantly, creates a championship culture.

In Texas, high school football is a big deal. I'm not one of those guys who think we put the laces in the balls, have better athletes or smarter coaches. I do believe we do it different than any other state.

Most head football coaches in Texas do not teach classes or have other duties. Many also serve as the athletic director for their school district. It is state law that anyone who coaches any student at one of our public schools must be a full-time employee of the district.

All schools in Texas have an 'athletic period' during the school day and in that athletic period all athletes are enrolled and coaches have the entire class time to prepare their teams. It is a year-round class and a big advantage we have here to prepare our teams both in-season and out-of-season.

Presently, I am the boy's athletic coordinator and head football coach at Grapevine High School in Grapevine, Texas. We have 1,900 students and 30 coaches. Our football staff consists of myself and 13 assistants.

PADUCAH DRAGONS

I haven't always had a staff so large. My first head coaching job was in Paducah, Texas in 1999. Paducah is a small West Texas farming community of 1,200 people. We had 120 in high school and 25 football players. My superintendent was a great one, John Ferguson. Mr. Ferguson wanted to win and knew change was required. I was his guy and he didn't worry about politics as much as allowing me to do what I needed to build a program of discipline. I arrived in May and it was 'step and fetch' time to get anything established while I could. We had only three weeks left in the school year and each day was extremely important to get some type of foundation set for the summer and fall.

Dragon Stadium - Paducah, Texas

I decided we would meet each morning before school and go over our basic scheme and make our plan for each afternoon.

We met from 6 - 7:30 a.m. My staff of three wasn't real excited about this. The first morning one of them was not there. The next morning he showed up, but a different coach was absent. The third morning was exactly like the first ... Coach A was gone again, but Coach B was there. When I asked where he was, Coach C said, "He's not real fired up about the changes, he isn't coming this morning." *Welcome to being in charge.*

Luckily for me, Mr. Ferguson had had enough. The fourth morning he made sure all were present and gave each of us a copy of a letter from our school attorney stating part of the coaching stipend earned was 'other duties assigned,' meaning not only would they be at our a.m. meetings, but they would also work in the summer helping to monitor the weight room (something else they weren't fired up about).

I will never forget how it made me feel to have a boss that 'had my back'. You never really know about someone until you go through 'the fire' with him/her. I had moved 300 miles to take my first head coaching job and was getting push-back from the guys I needed to get things going. Mr. Ferguson came through for me and established my authority. He was the 'anti-Jerry Jones,' so to speak.

Once all the drama ended and the season started it was football as normal and I was on cloud nine to have my chance to lead a program. We looked decent in both of our scrimmages, but the first game against Seymour was eye-opening. They manhandled us 36-7 on our field. They were so much more physical than we were I was just glad we didn't have a major injury other than my feelings getting hurt.

The next week we traveled north to Memphis, Texas but things weren't much better. The Cyclones thumped us 27-8. We didn't look overly coached. We had too many penalties and missed assignment. I didn't lose faith in my ability as a head coach, but I was wondering if anyone in Paducah was glad I was there.

We caught a break in our schedule and played five teams in a row that had less talent than we did. We got better each week. We eventually got in the playoffs and went on a run. We finished the season 10-4, advancing all the way to the state quarterfinals and I was named 1A Coach of the Year in the *Lubbock Avalanche Journal*.

We had only three seniors so the 2000 season looked promising. We played well and had a terrific season. We were 11-0 and ranked in the top three in the state all year before losing a nail biter 15-13 in the second round to another 11-0 squad, Rankin.

Paducah was a lot like Tenaha, where I grew up. It's a great small town that loves all its athletic teams. Having only three assistants and teaching three classes a day wasn't my long-term goal, so I started sending resumes hoping I could parlay two good years into a bigger school.

MASON PUNCHERS

In February 2001, I accepted the A.D. / head football job in Mason, Texas. Mason is one of the most beautiful towns in the entire state. It is in the Hill Country between Austin and San Angelo. It was a step up, career-wise. At the time, Mason was a 2A high school with an enrollment of 205. My football staff was huge compared to Paducah with a total of eight for middle school and high school. We had some great kids in Mason who played very hard. Mason has a lot of tradition. Football is important there and the guys I had did not want to let down the school or the community.

TELL THEM OVER AND OVER AND YOUR TEAM HAS CHANCE TO MAKE IT A SELF-FULL FILLING PROPHECY.

We were picked to finish last in the district by the state high school football 'Bible' — *Texas Football* magazine. We should have been, especially the way we played early in the season. We played five non-district games and were 0-5. After three district games we were 1-7 overall and 1-2 in district play. We had to win the last two games to get in the playoffs. We did it; we beat our rival Junction and then San Angelo Grape Creek to finish

3-2 in district and even had a little momentum.

We played a 9-1 McCamey squad at a neutral site in Eldorado, Texas. We nipped them 14-13. This is one of my fondest coaching memories. There is no way we should have won this game. Our guys believed and found a way.

Not sure how many teams have ever been 1-7 and won a playoff game, but I know there aren't many.

The 'Puncher Dome' – Mason, Texas

We told them every day we were going to make the playoffs and win a gold ball (trophy). Not one practice ended without me telling the team about our vision. As long as we were still in the playoff hunt the coaches believed and our guys believed.

WHEN YOU HAVE A CHANCE TO MOVE UP DON'T GET IMPATIENT

Be patient when deciding to move up the ladder (this is a

mistake I have made more than once). Mason was a step up from Paducah as far as players, coaches and pay, but it was too far from our families. We had two young children.

Russ was two and Katie was just a year old. Both sets of grandparents were six hours away. I should have been more patient and found a job closer to our homes in north and east Texas.

FAILURE IS PART OF THE PROCESS. WINNERS LOSE MORE THAN LOSERS LOSE. EVERY GREAT STORY HAS CRISIS THAT HAD TO BE OVERCOME. DON'T LET A SET BACK DERAIL YOU. YEARS LATER IT WILL BE PART OF YOUR TESTIMONY.

DeKALB BEARS

After one season in Mason, I wasn't looking to leave. A sporting goods salesman told me about a head coaching job opening in DeKalb, Texas. DeKalb was another 2A school, but larger than Mason with 300 in high school.

The athletes were also more suited to my spread offense. Without really knowing anyone there I got the job. We moved 400 miles across the state to the northeast corner of Texas.

Again, I got there in May with not much time to get things established before school was out.

I wasn't a good fit in DeKalb. The head coach I replaced had a much different style than I. His offense was much more conservative and he was very popular with his assistants. I got there late and all of them stayed on staff for the next school year.

Although they worked hard, our chemistry wasn't where it needed to be. Our season was outstanding; we won the district championship and advanced to the third round of the playoffs.

Obviously, my overall experience was one I could have lived without. There are winners and learners. I learned a lot from my time there.

I survived the summer in DeKalb and we came to a settlement just before the beginning of the school year in exchange for my resignation. I landed in Grapevine as the head freshman coach and social studies teacher. It was a great place to be while I healed and licked my wounds from my experience in DeKalb.

LONE OAK BUFFALOES

After 8 months in Grapevine the hiring committee of Lone Oak ISD invited me to be their next AD / head football coach. I was fired up to be an A.D. and head coach again, but also about being in Lone Oak again. Shannon and I built a house and stayed there six years. The entire family needed the stability and we were lucky to settle in Lone Oak.

Shannon taught at the middle school while Russ and Katie went from Pre-K thru most of elementary. We made some lifetime friends we still keep in contact with to this day.

> *"You earn your right to win games with effort and toughness. The game honors toughness."*
>
> **Brad Stevens**
> **Head Basketball Coach**
> **Boston Celtics**

Football is a big deal in Lone Oak. I was honored to coach guys there who 'couldn't live without it' and played their guts out each week.

Our teams were 50-20 during my tenure there. The last five years we qualified for the playoffs each year and won our first round game. We never could get over the hump and make a deep run, but I got to coach and work with lots of good people in Lone Oak.

By this time, I had been a head coach for ten years all at the 1A or 2A level. Small school coaches work their tails off. They all coach three sports and teach a full load of classes for usually less money than the big school guys. As athletic director I did not teach class, but there was plenty to get done. Every summer I would worry (pretty much on a daily basis) if the sprinklers were working properly. We would go to Greenville and borrow an industrial fertilizer spreader and pull behind a pickup to get some fertilizer down on the field. I mowed the game and practice fields. All of us divvyed up the painting on the game field.

The toughest role of athletic director in small schools is you are expected to be at most every athletic event; home and away. I tip my hat the coaches and their wives who allow them to do this. It is hard on coaches and their families to be gone as much as you have to be. If your basketball teams are playing fifty miles out of town on a Tuesday night then you kiss your wife and tell her you will try not to wake her up when you get home after 11 p.m. I am proud of my time in Paducah, Mason, DeKalb and Lone Oak. If need be I could poke a screw driver in the ground (for probably about 10 minutes) and find the corner of the end zone so we could figure out where to start on marking the field.

I always try and have a few guys on my staff now who have coached in a smaller school. These guys know how to work. They know how to fix a sprinkler, line a field, run the clock at a basketball game (for no pay), drive a bus, etc.

Buffalo Stadium – Lone Oak, Texas

DON'T WAIT FOR THE PERFECT OPPORTUNITY. IF THE STRUCTURE IS GOOD IT CAN BE DONE.

MESQUITE POTEET PIRATES

I was one of 18 who interviewed for the Mesquite Poteet head football position. It was a stressful process. There were six people in the room who asked five questions each so I answered 30 questions in 60 minutes. When I left, I had no idea how I had done, but I was mentally exhausted.

There was not a second round of interviews. I waited a couple of weeks without any word of where I stood in the process. The night before I was offered the job a friend who was 'in the know' told me Mesquite ISD had chosen someone else. He turned it down.

He wasn't the first one they asked who turned the job down. Before the interviews began I was warned to stay away from the job by a head coach who had faced Poteet the year before. He said it would be a bad career move and to stay more patient. Patience is not something I am known for.

I was ready for my chance at the 'big time.' I didn't care if I was the first, third or 10th choice. I was fired up to get going. Poteet was 1-19 the two seasons prior to my arrival in the spring of 2010, but structure and administration was sound so we were going to have a chance to build it correctly.

Mesquite Memorial Stadium – Mesquite, TX

Texas Football magazine had us picked to finish ninth in a nine-team district. Expectations were not high. There would be no pressure for a quick turnaround.

While I was hopeful, I didn't expect a lot of success that first year. Thank goodness our players believed enough for me. Just like in Mason, we told them every day we were going to be special. In the summer I wrote fake articles describing how we were going to make the playoffs and play in AT&T Stadium. I found an article describing how the Saints led the league in turnover margin so I rewrote it with having Poteet lead the state and used our guys names throughout. We were +25 in turnover margin for the year. I even wrote one that had us beating Hutto in bi-district. We beat them 21-20 in the first round. Set the vision, you never know if your team will 'over-believe'.

After we won our first two games I started telling them they would make a movie about this team. I described who would play all the coaches, with Will Farrell playing me.

We caught 'lightening in a bottle' and were one of the true turnaround teams in the state. We were one game away from playing for the state championship. Our season ended with a 12-3 record from 0-10 the year before.

> *"We didn't overachieve. We over-believed."*
>
> **Dabo Swinney**
> **Head Football Coach**
> **Clemson Tigers**

It was a true 'magic carpet ride'. This was the first place I got intentional with culture and leadership development. I knew we were taking over a program that lacked confidence. An assistant coach told me on my second day on the job, "the band makes fun of the football team here."

I knew then what my priority would be — to inject confidence in them. It was not an easy spring. Our only senior Division I prospect tore his ACL on the last play during one of our early practices. Our starting quarterback had quit before I arrived and didn't rejoin the team until the summer. In the spring game a freshman started at quarterback for both teams. I remember thinking, "this is not what I was thinking 4A ball would be."

IF YOU KNOW THE SITUATION IS NOT RIGHT FOR YOU DON'T EXPECT THEM TO CHANGE IT. WE ALL HAVE 'CLOSED-HAND BELIEFS'. IF YOU CANNOT THRIVE AT A SITUATION DO NOT STAY HOPING IT WILL GET BETTER.

A culture of confidence had to be created. We started fast in 2010 and our team gained momentum each week. The guys bought what we were selling. The strategies we used to develop the culture of TPW football gained traction because they were having success and enjoying the season.

PLANO EAST PANTHERS

After three very good years at Poteet I received a call from the athletic director for Plano ISD, who told me the head job at Plano East was open and he wanted to gauge my interest. Plano East is one of the largest high schools in the state with 6,000 students in grades 9-12. East has had several players play at major colleges and the NFL.

The pay raise would also be substantial. At first I wasn't interested, but the more I looked at the job, the more I started believing it was a job not many coaches would have the opportunity to get.

IT'S ABOUT RELATIONSHIPS

When I started in Paducah, getting enough players to practice was a struggle. Numbers would not be an issue at East. Four middle schools and two high schools (freshman and sophomore campuses) feed into Plano East. After doing the math I realized I would have 24 quarterbacks starting each

DON'T TAKE A JOB FOR THE PRESTIGE OR THE MONEY. IF YOU AREN'T THE RIGHT FIT YOU WILL BE FRUSTRATED. ASK, ASK, AND ASK MORE QUESTIONS DURING THE PROCESS.

week from grades 7 – 12. I was like a bug drawn to the light. I knew the system was different than most but figured I would get used to it so I took the job.

I quickly realized I didn't ask enough questions and those I did ask were the wrong ones. Needless to say, I was a bad fit.

'Lay in traffic' is a term we use a lot in Grapevine. We want guys to not want to let their coaches or their teammates down. This will only occur when you develop deep relationships with them. I believe you must start this as soon as possible. I asked the East coaches in the spring to make a depth chart for the next three years. They couldn't do it. It wasn't their fault at all, they just don't know our future players well enough.

The Plano system is a junior college model and a tough way to build relationships. The 9-10 campuses have different school colors and mascots as the senior high campuses. They have 'homecoming' at one of the 10th grade games. For a small town guy like me, it was frustrating. After one 5-5 season, I left for the more traditional high school setting.

GRAPEVINE MUSTANGS

In 2014, I accepted the head football position in Grapevine. Again, it was a program with little success ... a rebuilding project. We struggled during our first year. We took baby steps and got better as the season progressed, but our culture wasn't in place. We finished 3-8.

We would have to turn the program the old-fashioned way — in the offseason. 2015 was much better, we were 8-3 and much improved. We were tougher, played with a purpose and had great team chemistry. Our culture was 100% better. There is no better sense of accomplishment than changing the culture of a program. Both of these were different situations and had a different timeline, but there are many similarities that I believe will work for any situation.

After our initial season we got very intentional with developing toughness. We wrestled, we ran, we implemented a very tough boot camp. Some decided they didn't want to pay the price, but we pressed forward with the ones who committed.

I knew we had to 'tear it down to the studs' and build our program back with guys who couldn't live without it. We had around 25 players decide it wasn't for them. It was tough. Every few days another player would say, "Coach, can I talk to you?" My stomach would drop. I knew what was coming, but I also knew it was the right thing. We had to change the culture and make it one based on toughness.

It was obvious to me we had two choices: slowly change things and be frustrated with guys who could live without football or have a 'come to Jesus' offseason and rebuild it with guys who paid a heavy price. As gut-wrenching as it was to have guys quit every few days, it made me that much more proud for the guys who stuck it out and enjoyed our turnaround season this past year.

Mustang Stadium – Grapevine, Texas

I'm just finishing my third spring at Grapevine. We are a work in progress, but we're on our way to being a relevant 5A program in the area and state. We have a great system in place to overachieve.

We have first period athletics each morning and get our work done early. After school, our guys come back to lift weights and watch film. All 14 coaches are allowed to work with players on our freshman, junior varsity and varsity teams. I'm proud of what we are accomplishing.

I have coached at schools from the smallest classification to the largest. My family and I have lived all over the state of Texas. No place has been perfect, but all have been great in their own way and I've grown from each. My wife, Shannon, and I laugh and/or cringe when we reflect back on all our moves. It's been hard on our family.

The one thing it has done is give me different labs to learn how to develop culture and leadership.

"WE CAN PUT HIS ACL BACK IN WHEN THE SEASON IS OVER."

"Coach, let me run 24 Smash one more time."

Manuel Gonzales was our tailback in Mason. This was back when we were under center and had two running backs some of the time. He was a hard-nosed, tough kid (he was also our starting linebacker). In Week 9, Manuel tore his ACL during a big win against Junction (this was the team that started 1-7).

Because Manuel was a senior, our team doctors said they could remove the ligament, let him rest two weeks and he could play again if we made it to the second round. Once we were eliminated from the playoffs, they would go back in and re-attach the ACL. They said it would be uncomfortable, but if he could tolerate the pain he could play.

Manuel was one of our team captains so this was great news for all of us. He was a leader before I understood the significance of being 'on purpose' and developing them. We knew he would not be 100%, but his presence would be huge if we could make it long enough to get him back.

PHYSICAL TOUGHNESS MEASURES WHAT YOU ARE CAPABLE OF DOING.

MENTAL TOUGHNESS MEASURES WHETHER YOU WILL ACTUALLY DO IT.

As I mentioned earlier we had one of the biggest upsets in the state in the first round of the playoffs. This took us to the second round where Manuel was cleared to play. His lateral movement was still not very good, but we were hoping he would have a presence playing middle linebacker against a big Coahoma squad that ran the ball 90% of the time.

It didn't take long to realize we were out-matched. Coahoma was good and we struggled to stop them. We got down big early and the outcome was never in doubt.

Manuel played as much as he could. He was in pain and the score was out of hand. Every few series he would go back in and play until he couldn't take it anymore.

Although we threw the ball 43 times in the game, we ran the ball to eat the clock in the last few minutes. Manuel came to me with tears in his eyes and asked, "Can I run 24 Smash one more time?" It was our 'hat rack' play, the play he had ran 158 times during the season. He was good at it. It's an inside toss that allows for a cutback and Manuel had a great knack for seeing the cutback. Manuel limped out onto the field, caught the toss and like he had done so many times before, cut it back and got four yards. It was the most awesome 24 Smash I had ever seen. Manuel was a real tough guy who wanted to go out his way ... by running his play.

When I talk to my teams about what tough is, sometimes I tell the story about a player playing his last game, with no ACL, wanting to run the toss just one more time. I have coached a lot of tough players, but Manuel Gonzales was one of the toughest and one of my favorites.

CHAPTER 1 REVIEW
CAREER LESSONS FROM MY JOURNEY

- TOUGH PEOPLE WIN. Being a coach is not for the faint of heart. Be ready to have a few scars.

- There is no great story without struggle. Your hard times will be your testimony later.

- Great programs have great support from above. Make sure you will be supported by your administration on the things that are important to you.

- Brainwash them. Tell your team every day the vision and they will go above and beyond to make it happen. Most things are self-fulfilled prophecies. Give them a big goal and talk about it over and over.

- Make sure you are the right fit. Do not take a job for the pay raise. Investigate each opportunity as thoroughly as possible. Many jobs look much better on the outside than they do on the inside.

- When you know you are not the right fit, don't stay. Each job has its positives and negatives. Find a place you can thrive and your program can overachieve.

CHAPTER #2

CREATING CORE VALUES

> *"When I interview anyone for a position within the Ohio State athletic department I always ask them what four personal core values they live by."*
>
> **Gene Smith**
> **Athletic Director**
> **Ohio State University**

"Coach, our guys don't wear their championship rings, ever. They don't wear shirts or anything that says National Champions. It's in the past. We are all about the process and focused on getting better today. We don't look back."

I was sitting across from Jamar Cain, defensive line coach at North Dakota State University. The Bisons are the reigning 5-time FCS National Champions.

"If one of our guys is not going all out, 100%, one of our guys will grab him and fix it. I don't coach effort here. When I am watching film with the defensive line, a veteran in the room corrects a mistake before I can. We have the most unselfish players I have ever seen. It's the greatest place to coach because it is all about team and tough."

I have a great job. I get to talk to college coaches on their winter and spring recruiting trips. After we talk about our prospective recruits I pick their brains and ask them about the culture of their program.

Coach Cain and I spoke for a while about the culture of the NDSU program. Another great standard they have is their 'Champions Room.' It's a special room with memorabilia, leather couches, big screen TV's, etc. It's an honor to be allowed to go into that room.

Only players and coaches who have won a conference or national championship are allowed in. After the season is over (and ANOTHER championship has been won) the veterans stand outside the room and enthusiastically invite the new members in. How does NDSU create this culture? It doesn't happen by accident. It happens 'on purpose.'

We are paid to read. Anyone in a leadership role should be an avid reader. The last few years I have begun to read more and more. While I have read some great books, Pete Carroll's 'Win Forever' is at the top of my list. It's an amazing read.

CORE VALUES ARE THE COMPASS FOR YOUR PROGRAM. TO HAVE A TRUE CULTURE YOU MUST HAVE CORE VALUES TO GUIDE YOUR DAY-TO-DAY.

Coach Carroll talks about fascinating his players every day. He discusses how he developed his basic coaching philosophies after he was fired by the New England Patriots. His core values are a big theme of the book. I decided after reading it we would have core values at Grapevine during my first year in 2014.

I borrowed a couple of the ones Coach Carroll uses with his Win Forever organization: 'always compete' and 'be early'. We always preach 'tough' so that was one of our values also. I heard Coach Bill Curry speak in the summer and he talked about a word that meant "greatness of spirit." The word is "**magnanimitas**." I had a couple of door wraps made with our core values on them, but no one else had any input on our core values, especially the players.

Did we have core values that year? Not so much. Other than when they walked through those doors to enter the field house they never saw or talked about them. Not only did our guys not have any say on what the values were, we never checked for understanding to see if they knew them. We sure didn't define any of them. I read a book, heard a lecture and came up with some core values. I even chose a Latin word none of them could spell, pronounce and much less care about!

Enter Brian Cain of Peak Performance.

Brian asked me if I had core values for my program. Sure I did! But even though I could proudly tell him what those core values were, he pointed out that they were nowhere to be found.

"If they're important," he said, "they should be everywhere and talked about daily."

I was embarrassed and he was 100% correct. I had some core values that meant something to me, but that was about it.

Brian spoke at our athletic staff development a couple of weeks before. I have always had a growth mindset and was fired up to have him help me for a few sessions. The core value system he helped to create was one of the biggest ingredients for our turnaround season.

When creating core values for your team, ask each team member to give you one word he wants the team to be known for. What do we want to define ourselves as?

We did this with a Google survey. It was very simple and results came in quickly. I led our guys in the direction I wanted them to go by asking 'please list the one value you want our program to be known by'. For example: tough, compete (two values I knew had to be on our list). I compiled all the words/values and made a list of the top five. I also add two more that I knew I would emphasize and wanted to be a part of our culture.

Our core values are:

Energy & Tempo - **Compete** - **Toughness**

Family & Appreciation - **Discipline**

Finish - **Pay Day**

Because they were allowed to participate in the process of creating our core values, our guys felt like they had some ownership. This helped with the 'buy in' tremendously.

Although there are other ways to organize your core values, we decided to assign each of ours to a day of the week. This is a 'no-brainer' idea to me, having a day of the week where you focus on one core value each day.

In most every sport, Monday can be a sluggish practice. After the weekend it can be a challenge to get them going in 90+ degree temperatures. For this reason, we assigned 'Energy and Tempo' to Monday. We want to get our week off to a great start by emphasizing high energy.

'5 MINUTE RULE' – WHEN SOMEONE COMES TO YOUR PRACTICE THEY WILL SEE WHAT YOUR TRUE CORE VALUES ARE WITHIN FIVE MINUTES.

We keep score of our group and team periods on Tuesdays so 'Compete' was a natural choice. Toughness Wednesday, Family and Appreciation Thursday and Discipline Friday rounded out our values. More games are lost than won due to mental errors and lack of discipline so we focus on discipline on game days.

That leaves two core values I added to the list: Finish and Pay Day. I love the concept of 'finish.' Playing through the whistle and being relentless every play. Game Day is also the time to have fun. You've put in the work. It's time to get paid ... Pay Day.

We still needed a way to bring home the message and memorize our core values. We did this through a hand routine. Each finger on our hand represents a core value and a day of the week.

Our hand routine:

Energy and Tempo Monday: Thumb – hold it high like 'Gig 'em Aggies' and make a circular motion (stirring the pot)

Competition Tuesday: Index finger – point at opponent and move back and forth for 'Me vs You'

Toughness Wednesday: Middle finger – point at temple and hip back and forth. Temple = mental toughness and Hip = physical toughness

Family and Appreciation Thursday: Ring finger – slide opposite thumb and index finger up and down ring finger to represent wedding ring (love)

Discipline Friday: Pinky – point pinky at sternum. 'Count on me'

Finish: Hold fist in the air

<u>Pay Day</u>: Slam fist down

Finish and Pay Day are not officially assigned a day, but are tied to game day. We must finish and we must be the most excited team on the field because it is payday!

Each player memorized, stood in front of the team and recited our core values with the hand routine. They wouldn't get their helmet decals until they could do it. Having them do this routine was a great addition to the building of our culture, our guys were getting it. They were involved in the process of selecting our core values and we made sure each player knew them. Compared to my lame attempt at the year before, we were way ahead of the game.

The next step in creating your core values is to have a CREDO. Our credo is our core values defined (have to define to achieve). Again, we did this as a team. This time we just listed them in a team meeting and all players and coaches came up with a short definition for each value.

The Grapevine Football Mustang Credo:

<u>Energy / Tempo</u> - Relentless effort. We attack with tenacity and make their butts quit.

<u>Competition</u> - 1-0 mentality. We are 1 play scorpions who always compete.

<u>Toughness</u> - Comfortable being uncomfortable. We impose our will and dominate with toughness.

FAMILY & Appreciation - We value others above our selves. Build others up and are a team of foxhole brothers.

Discipline – Always doing what needs to be done. We chop wood and carry water everyday.

Finish - Doing more than what is expected. We are a freight train that terrorizes with our finish.

Pay Day – Starving for greatness. We are crumb eaters who get what we earn while leaving no doubt about the TPW way!

To get every member of the team to do our hand routine and say the credo was going to take it to the next level. Every one of our guys did this also.

We told them we would put names on the back of their jerseys once all recited the credo. It was great to have guys come up and do it in front of the team.

SELL YOUR CORE VALUES

We sell our core values and credo as often as we can. I had posters printed with one of our players on it and the core values on his gloves. It looks amazing.

We gave a poster to each player, our middle school players and GHS teachers. We walked downtown Grapevine and asked businesses to put them in their windows.

We have two TV's up in the varsity locker room. We have a slideshow on both of them that scroll continuously. I put our core values on the side of our travel bags, our credo on the back of our playoff t-shirts, anywhere and everywhere we can.

WIN THE NATIONAL ANTHEM

We honor America and the soldiers who have protected us in the past and are protecting us now before each game. We align in numerical order, helmet under the right arm and left hand touching the shoulder pad of player in front.

At the end of the anthem all hands go up in the air into a fist ('finish' position).

After a respectful pause a captain yells, "Mustangs," then the entire team shouts "Payday" and drops their fist.

JACK AND LEO

Jack and Leo were teammates on a state championship football team.

Jack was an All-American linebacker. He was one of the most popular guys in school. He was smart and handsome. Jack went on to play at Texas Tech and had a great career. Leo played receiver and was an extremely hard worker. He never started a game, but was voted captain his senior year.

Twenty years later their graduating class was having a reunion. Jack shows up and is looking for Leo. Finally, 30 minutes later he sees him, they hug, sit down and have a great visit.

Eventually, Jack tells Leo, "I was always so jealous of you." Leo said, "makes no sense to me. You were All-American, MVP, girls always wanted to hang around you, reporters talked to you, it had to be a great experience."

Jack said, "Yes all that is true, but the team voted you captain. The one thing I wanted most was to be our team captain. I never could understand it while we were playing together. I finally asked the coach on the last day of school, 'Why did the team pick Leo captain instead of me?'"

Coach said, "Jack, you are one of the best players I have ever coached. You were definitely one of the best players in the state this year. Leo had nothing on you, except he wanted the TEAM to be the best in the state. Leo would stay late in the weight room. He would stay after practice and work extra with the other receivers. He would give players a ride home if they needed. Whatever anyone needed Leo would do. He was all about our core values."

"You wanted to be the best player on the team. Leo wanted to be the best player FOR the team."

"Your personal core values determine who you are, and a company's core values ultimately define the company's character and brand.
For individuals, character is destiny.
For organizations, culture is destiny. "

Tony Hsieh

CHAPTER 2 REVIEW
CREATING CORE VALUES

☐ What do you want your program to be about? When people visit and watch your practices it will be known quickly.

☐ Core values guide your program. Great teams have a standard that all players know.

☐ Allow your players to be a part of creating your core values.

☐ To memorize something associate an object and have a routine.

☐ Make sure all players can recite not only core values, but your credo as well.

☐ Post your core values everywhere you can. Make your field house a core value factory. Sell them constantly.

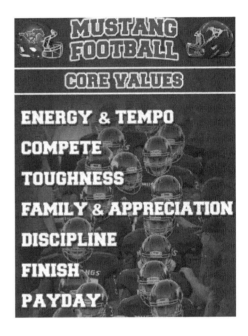

MUSTANG FOOTBALL
CORE VALUES
ENERGY & TEMPO
COMPETE
TOUGHNESS
FAMILY & APPRECIATION
DISCIPLINE
FINISH
PAYDAY

CHAPTER #3

THE 4-QUARTER PROCESS

> *"The process is what you have to do day in and day out to be successful. Eliminate all the things outside your control and focus on daily improvement. Focus on the process."*
>
> **Nick Saban**
> **Head Coach**
> **Alabama Crimson Tide**

Tom was the best homebuilder in the city, maybe even the entire state. He was known for his attention to detail and excellent work. His bosses always gave him the most demanding homes and clients because they knew he would produce. Tom's work had become legendary due to his dedication to the process and his relentless devotion to keep learning, even late into his career.

Tom was ready to retire. He'd been building homes for more than 40 years and was ready to start the next chapter of his life. He and his wife were eager to travel and spend more time with the grandkids.

Tom gave his two-week notice to his bosses. In a tired voice, he thanked them for allowing him to serve, but told them he was ready to move on.

One of his bosses said, "Tom, we are forever indebted to you and what you have done for our company. When you began working here we were struggling to make it and now we are one of the top builders in Texas. We can't thank you enough, but we have one last favor to ask. Could you build one more home? It's for a special client and all of us agreed it requires your magic touch."

Tom was frustrated. He would have to postpone his retirement for a few months. He would even have to cancel a trip they had planned to Hawaii to celebrate his retirement. But, like the good soldier he had always been, Tom reluctantly agreed to build the house.

The problem was Tom agreed with his head, but his heart wasn't in it. That hands-on approach that had been his signature through the entire building process was not happening. Instead of selecting the finest materials by hand and overseeing every detail, Tom delegated these task to others.

This last house was different for Tom. He viewed it as an obligation instead of an opportunity. He let things slip through the cracks. Sure, the home was structurally sound and would pass inspection, but it was not a signature "Tom-built" home. It lacked the "wow" of the homes he had built for the last 40 years. It was a half-hearted effort at best.

Tom knew this was far from his best work, but he was ready to move on. He was doing this last project as a favor for his bosses. This phase of his life was not appealing to him. Retirement was all he could think of.

After four months passed, the home was finished. Tom went back to his boss, telling him, "I did what you asked.

Now I am asking, one last time, for your blessing to retire."

"Thank you, Tom!", said his boss. After he inspected the home he said, "Now we just have one more thing."

"EVERYTHING MATTERS" His boss reached out and handed Tom the keys with a small ribbon around them. "We are so grateful for you, Tom. This home is a gift of our appreciation."

Tom's heart sank. Little did he know, the whole time he was building HIS house. He was shocked and embarrassed.

If only he had known, he would've cared so much more. He would've used only the finest materials and would have overseen the smallest of detail. If he had known the consequences he would have demanded more from himself. But now, it was too late.

Everything matters. There are no unimportant days. To be great during your season you must 'build your house' during the nine months of offseason. Once the season rolls around it will be too late.

YEARLY CALENDAR

At Grapevine, our nine months are planned out into four quarters in addition to football season. Football season takes care of itself. Our edge is how we break down the months in addition to the season.

The 12 months and 4 quarters of Grapevine football:

Fall camp
Football season
Quarter 1 – December and January (hopefully just January!)
Quarter 2 – February through April
Quarter 3 – Spring football
Quarter 4 – Summer strength and conditioning

> **"The difference in something good and something great is attention to detail."**
>
> **Charles Swindoll**

Our four-quarter system allows us to be intentional with short-term focus and growth. In each quarter we have a motto.

Our guys define our motto in their own words and tape on an index card at the top of their locker.
We also have them identify a one word focus for the quarter.

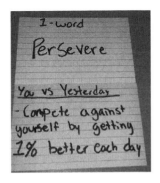

> **"There is no hope for a better yesterday. Make today great."**
>
> **Dabo Swinney**
> **Head Coach**
> **Clemson Tigers**

Examples of motto's we have used in the past:

Quarter 1 (Dec-Jan) - Grapevine Strong / Ring the Bell

Quarter 2 (Feb-April) - Discipline Wins

Quarter 3 (Spring ball) - You vs. Yesterday

Quarter 4 (summer) - "4th and 1" / Stronger Together / Kaizen (continuous improvement) - 1% warrior

Football season - 'Earn Your Badge' / Lock the Gate / Move the Mountain / All In / Swing the Big Axe

OUR BRAND

TPW - "Tough People Win" is our brand and a constant each year. When I took over at Lone Oak High School in 2004 I wanted to create a culture of toughness.

I knew we wouldn't always be the most athletic team on the field, but we could always be the toughest. I decided on the acronym "TPW" and have taken it with me to every school since.

I love it because it doesn't require talent or 'measureables' to be tough. The #1 factor in success in life is not intelligence or ability. It's grit. Grit is courage, resolve and strength of character. Toughness is a form of grit.

We sell toughness every day in every aspect of our program. I'm proud of how our program in Grapevine has transformed into one where toughness is a major ingredient. Later, in Chapter 6, I'll go in-depth on how we work to develop toughness and grit.

> *"Average leaders have a quote. Good leaders have a plan. Great leaders have a system."*
>
> **Urban Meyer**
> **Head Coach**
> **Ohio State Buckeyes**

MISSION STATEMENTS

In addition to our core values we have a mission statement for TPW football. Ours is: "To build quality young men to be champions for life through football."

A mission statement is important because it states what your program does, what your program's mission is and why it exists.

A mission statement should be succinct, short and to the point. Like your core values, all coaches should be able to recite it.

Not only do we have a mission statement for our program, we also have them for each critical unit. Each coach involved with any of the areas should be able to articulate the mission of the unit.

Grapevine football mission statements:

<u>Character development</u> - we will pour into our guys every day. We realize our responsibility and are honored to help grow them into men.

<u>Academics</u> - graduation with options for the next level are paramount. We will actively monitor, tutor and encourage our guys to be great students.

<u>Recruiting</u> - to help our young men play at the next level by going the extra mile for them.

<u>Community Service</u> - "Mustangs Serving Others" Servant leadership is the most important leadership. We will teach and emphasize regularly.

<u>Sub-varsity teams</u> - all coaches will give our younger, developmental players the same effort and passion as our varsity players. All players deserve great coaching.

<u>Kicking game</u> - to be different, but sound at all times. We will get the edge with our special forces with appropriate, intense time spent for each unit.

<u>Defense</u> - to be the most sound, physical and swarming defense in the state. Punish the offense and create takeaways.

<u>Offense</u> - to play with a 'hair on fire' tempo and score points with machine-like execution.

VISION STATEMENT

Different from a mission statement, a vision statement identifies the results you want.

Why are vision statements important? Results matter. Coaching is a results-driven profession. Never has there been less patience for head coaches than there is now.

It is alarming each season when we see coaches who have great overall records at a school or professional team, but have a couple of bad years and are shown the door out.

> **"Where there is no vision the people perish."**
> **Proverbs 29:18**

While we all want to make more money, sometimes the higher the salary the shorter the rope when wins don't come quickly.

Top-flight programs have a clear sense of where they are going because a true leader provides the vision.

The author, Ken Blanchard, talks about the importance of vision when he relates a story about his dad retiring fairly young as a captain from the Navy.

Ken asks, "Dad, do you regret retiring so young? If you would have stay you would have had a great chance to make Admiral."

"Not really, son. I hate to say it, but I liked the wartime Navy a lot better than the peacetime Navy. Not that I liked to fight, but in wartime we knew what our purpose was and what we were trying to accomplish.

The problem with the peacetime Navy is no one what we are supposed to be doing. As a result, too many leaders think their job is to make others feel unimportant."

The Grapevine football vision statement:

To do things better than they have ever been done before through relationships, accountability and culture.

To build a program that consistently competes for championships and is known statewide for class and toughness.

"Success isn't always about greatness. It's about consistency."

Dwayne 'The Rock' Johnson

ALI'S BIKE

"I am going to 'whup' whoever stole my bike", a 12-year old Cassius Clay told a police officer in Louisville, Kentucky. Cassius' family was poor. He had worked odd jobs and saved his money for almost a year. After all that time, he had saved enough to buy a bicycle. It was red and he loved it.

Muhammad Ali was in born in Louisville in 1942. In the 1960 Olympics, then Cassius Clay won the gold medal. Four years later, as a 7-1 underdog, he defeated Sonny Liston to become the heavyweight champion of the world. A star was born.

In the 1960's and 70's, Ali was the greatest fighter in the world. He was a worldwide phenomenon. "The Greatest of All Time."

It all started because his red and white bike was stolen. Cassius was in a store with some friends looking for free candy and popcorn. When they came outside, his bike was gone and he was fuming mad. As he was looking for the nearest police officer, he was told to go to the basement of a building nearby. As fate would have it, the police officer was also boxing trainer.

"Before you go off trying to fight someone over this bike, I suggest to build up that scrawny body of yours and learn how to box", said officer Joe Martin.

Cassius was all of 89 pounds at the time. With Martin's help, he became very good very fast. He moved through the junior rankings quickly. Each time he entered the ring he was on a mission and had a vision.

"I told myself the guy in the other corner was the one who stole my bike. That bike was everything to me.

Even as I became a professional every time I entered the ring I worked myself up by saying 'this guy stole my bike and I am going to punish him for it'...and I did."

CHAPTER 3 REVIEW
THE 4-QUARTER PROCESS

☐ Break your off-season into 4 quarters to refine your focus into manageable blocks.

☐ Have your players create a '1 word focus' for each quarter.

☐ Have a motto for each quarter and have players define in their own words.

☐ What is your brand? Create a constant brand for your players and community to identify with.

☐ Mission statements define what your program does.

☐ Vision statements define what your program wants to accomplish in the future.

CHAPTER 4

LESSON #1 – ENERGY & TEMPO

"What are you selling today? Are you selling positive energy or are you selling negative energy? Are you affecting everyone else in a positive way or a negative way?"

Nick Saban
Head Coach
Alabama Crimson Tide

The year was 1907 and Frank Bettger was a minor league baseball player in the Tri-state league in Johnstown, Pennsylvania. That is, until his manager fired him.

Frank said the best thing that ever happened to him was going to the manager to ask why. He was fired because he was lazy.

"You drag yourself around the field like a veteran who has been playing 20 years."

Bettger tried to talk himself back onto the team saying he was nervous, scared and was trying to hide this from the crowd.

"Frank, it'll never work. That's what's holding you down. When you leave here, for heaven's sake, wake up and put some enthusiasm into your work."

He was making $175 a month in Johnstown. After being

run off, Frank went to Chester, Pennsylvania in the Atlantic League and made $25 a month.

Although he wasn't enthusiastic about the pay, he did decide to take his manager's advice and act enthusiastic. After just three days an old ball player, Danny Meehan, asked, "Frank, what in the world are you doing in a rank, bush league like this?" Bettger replied, "Danny, I would go anywhere if I could get a tryout in a better league."

The next week, Danny induced New Haven, Connecticut to give Frank a tryout. No one knew Bettger so no one knew of his reputation for being lazy. He made up his mind to be the most enthusiastic player ever seen in the New England League. He figured if he could establish the reputation he would have to live up to it.

From the minute he stepped on the field, he played like a man electrified. Frank said, "I acted like I was alive and had a million batteries inside me. I threw the ball around the diamond so fast and so hard it almost knocked our infielders' hands apart. Once, apparently trapped, I slid into third base with so much energy and force that the third baseman fumbled the ball and I was able to score an important run. Yes, it was all a show, an act I was putting on. The thermostat that day read 100 degrees. I wouldn't have been surprised if I had dropped from heat stroke that day."

Did it work? It worked better than Frank or anyone else could have imagined. According to Frank three things happened:

1. His energy almost entirely overcame his fear. In fact, he credits his nervousness as working for him. It helped him play better than he ever had before.
2. His enthusiasm affected the other players on the team. They became high-energy also.
3. Instead of dropping from the heat he felt invigorated. When the game was over he felt better than he ever had before.

The New Haven newspaper the next day called him "Pep" Bettger.

"This new player, Bettger, has a barrel of enthusiasm. He inspired our boys. They not only won the game, but looked better than at any time this season."

Within 10 days Frank had went from making $25 a month to now $185 a month at New Haven ... more than he was making in Johnstown, and all because of his commitment to being high-energy. Three weeks prior he had been fired for his laziness. Now he was known as "Pep!!"

"I didn't know any more about baseball than I did before. Nothing but determination to act enthusiastically increased my income 700% in 10 days!"

Two years later he was playing third base for the St. Louis Cardinals.

"What caused all this to happen? Enthusiasm alone did it. Nothing but enthusiasm."

HIRE HIGH-ENERGY COACHES

We are a student-athlete-based program at Grapevine. Our goal is for our field house to be a place they can't live without. We feel like we have a great vibe here. It's hard to describe exactly what having a great vibe is, but energy is a big part.

How do you create a high-energy program? First, you emphasize and make it a priority. Secondly, you hire high-energy coaches. When hiring coaches, if there was one thing I could do every time, it would be to watch him coach during practice. I would also love to see how they interact with the players in the field house.

> *"Practice being excited. "*
>
> **Bill Parcells**
> **Former NFL Head Coach**

I would interview their position players. Do they bring energy? I want guys who are the most excited coaches on the field. The energy then has a chance to flow from the coach to the player.

Bettger figured it out. High energy and enthusiasm are not optional for greatness. He changed his life because he started being the most energetic player on the field. We can't rely on having a Frank Bettger to have a high-energy practice. Bettger was the exception.

If our field house is going to be a place they can't live without, they must know we are fired up they are there. With our class schedule, we practice in the mornings. The only way we can have a great vibe is having coaches who are genuinely happy to see our players each morning when they arrive.

I chose to assign energy and tempo with Monday to emphasize getting our week off to a great start. One way we use our core values is to have a system to organize pre- and post-practice talks to the team.

On Monday, when I speak to the team, energy and playing fast are two of the main topics. It's not our opponent for the week. It's about us. As long as we focus on us and having the best Monday practice we can have, we'll be fine.

- LEADERS CREATE CULTURE

- CULTURE DRIVES BEHAVIOR

- BEHAVIOR PRODUCES RESULTS

We recognize after practice the players who had the most energy. With that being said, energy must always come from the top down.

LEADERS SET THE EXAMPLE

The head coach must model energy and enthusiasm at practice.

This attitude must run through the assistant coaches as well. Coaches are the climate-setters at practice and games. 17-year-olds can have lots of drama in their life. Trey may have failed a test. Zack's girl may have called it quits.

THE TIME OUR PLAYERS SPEND WITH US SHOULD BE THE BEST PART OF THEIR DAY.

Matt's parents may be splitting up. They go through so much these days.

We must be the #1 source of energy for the program. Our guys should always be able to count on their coaches. Coaches love the game; we invest a lot of time to prepare a great practice schedule.

We must also be energy 'igniters'. If the coaches are enthusiastic their players will be enthusiastic. If you have ever been to a college practice you will see coaches burning calories. They are constantly moving and coaching. They are high-energy.

> "The strongest form of motivation is exhortation. Everyone wants to be encouraged. Everyone wants a support group. Find the things they do well and have a pep rally."
>
> Bill McCartney
> Former Head Coach
> Colorado Buffaloes

ENERGY IS BEING POSITIVE

This book isn't about science and theory. I'm not smart enough for that. It's about specific strategies to create culture and become a better leader. But, when discussing positive coaching, the 5:1 ratio seems to be the gold standard.

This ratio might derive from research in the 1970's by Robert and Evelyn Kirkhart. They found that children in classrooms thrived when the ratio of feedback was five parts positive to one part constructive. In contrast, children sunk into despair if the ratio fell down to 2:1 or 1:1.

More recent research from the business world also supports the 5:1 ratio. A study of 60 leadership teams was printed in the Harvard Business Review. Academic consultants Emily Heaphy and Marcial Losada found the ratio of positive to negative comments the participants made to one another.

The average ratio for the highest-performing teams was 5.6, that is, nearly six positive comments for every negative one. The medium-performance teams averaged 1.9, almost twice as many positive comments than negative ones.

However, the average for the low-performing teams, at 0.36 to 1, was almost three negative comments for every positive one.

John Wooden, arguably the greatest coach of all time, had his practices videoed and analyzed at one point during his career at UCLA. Researchers broke down every word that came out of Coach Wooden's mouth and found that 87% of them were positive. That is very close to the magic 5:1 ratio.

Positive wins. It wins in sports and the corporate world. If positive wins with adults, then it's even more critical for us to remember this when dealing with school-aged athletes. Sometimes we do 'get after them,' so to speak.

Anyone who has ever coached with me knows I will lose my cool at times. I am working on this!!!

When it does happen we must be intentional about lifting the player up afterwards. When I really get on someone I will make sure I go put my arm around him later and make sure he knows I love him and am trying to get him to be his best.

I do believe the more we can be positive the better. When Katie was in second grade, she walked over to Poteet everyday with my son from their elementary right across the street. They would wait in my office for my wife to come pick them up.

One day she asked Shannon if I yelled at my players a lot. Shannon said, "Not too often, only when he gets mad at them."

"He was real mad at them today," Katie told her.

I chuckle at this story, but it hits home. It's not the way to do it. Practices must be intense, but intense can be positive. Science proves it has to be for maximum results.

COACH EVERY PLAY

Early in my career I was lucky to work for some great head coaches. One of the things I learned quickly was to give feedback after every play. I don't understand how a coach can watch a play and not say something to one of his players when it's over. We go fast so we talk fast, but if you visited one of our practices, you would hear all of our coaches praising or correcting constantly.

I once worked for a head coach who wouldn't allow us to wear sunglasses at practice. He said the players must be able to see your eyes when you coach them. While I understand the thought behind this, we wear sunglasses in Grapevine. The afternoon sun can be damaging to our eyes.

Early on in my career, a friend was on a staff where coaches could not put their hands in their pockets. I remember thinking this was a little over the top. Now, it seems so absurd someone would put their hands in their pockets at practice that it would go without saying.

A college coach and I were talking about the subject this spring and he told me Coach Gary Pinkel, recently retired at Missouri, had this rule for his assistants during practice. You could do two things with your hands; use them when you are coaching or put them behind your back when you are not coaching. I tried this the next day at spring ball. It felt odd to stand there with my hands behind my back. It made me intentional about always coaching. Good stuff, indeed.

> *"Preach the word; be prepared in season and out of season; correct, rebuke, and encourage with great patience and careful instruction."*
>
> **2 Timothy 4:2**

Whatever you have to do to remind yourself to coach every play, do it. Coaching is a high-energy job. Your players are busting their tails for you. They deserve to be coached the same way. Correct, rebuke and encourage!!!

ENERGY IS FAST

High energy and high tempo go hand in hand. It's impossible to go fast without enthusiasm. People with great attitudes rarely move slow.

I'm not good at slow. My impatience has caused me problems my entire life because I have made decisions too quickly. I would rather be an hour early than a minute late.

My impatience benefits my team as far as pace of practice is concerned. We go fast and don't have any wasted minutes, or seconds for that matter. I don't understand practices or workouts that are not 100 mph and "full throttle."

> *"Nobody ever defended anything successfully. There is only attack and attack and attack some more."*
>
> **General George S. Patton**

General George S. Patton was the most feared allied general by the Germans in WWII. He moved more men; conquered more ground in less time any general in the war.

Patton was known as a commander whose troops were swift.

"We shall attack and attack until we are exhausted, and

then we shall attack again," he told his troops before the initial landings in North Africa, thereby summarizing the military creed that won victory after victory along the long road that led from Casablanca to the heart of Germany.

It was when Patton led his beloved Third Army on the Western Front that he staked out his strongest claims to military greatness. In 10 months, his armor and infantry roared through six countries — France, Belgium, Luxembourg, Germany, Czechoslovakia and Austria.

It crossed the Seine, the Loire, the Moselle, the Saar, the Rhine, the Danube and a score of lesser rivers; captured more than 750,000 Nazis and killed or disabled 500,000 others.

When Patton was a young officer at West Point he trained to be a tank commander. At one point they had a competition between units. The instructors split them up into two teams and put them on opposite ends of a large 'battlefield.'

The winning team would capture a flag located in the middle of the field. Patton commanded the 'blue' team and as they were advancing the formation in a large area, he had a decision to make ... go right up a hill or go left through a small opening in a small forest.

Patton decided to go left. It was a mistake and his tank was 'destroyed' or put out of the competition. The majority of his tanks advanced and captured the flag. Patton was distraught. He thought for not 'surviving' the maneuver his instructors would grade him down. Instead, they praised him.

They were happy he made a decision and moved. Just sitting there and figuring it out would be the worst thing he could have done. All would have been sitting ducks. Although going through the trees would have been the better decision, at least he made a decision by moving. When in doubt ... ATTACK!

Speed is king. The world loves speed. Amazon is working hard to figure out how to deliver packages within hours of orders in major cities. We have all heard about the proposed use of drones, but they are also currently in the process of developing a system to hire Uber drivers to deliver packages. When drivers are not on a regular Uber call to pick up a passenger, they can deliver an Amazon product. It's about who can deliver the fastest.

We have three speeds at Grapevine — warm-up, teaching and game speed. Our practices are broken into many small segments of 2-5 minutes in length. None of our coaches gets bored during one of our practices.

Our team chaplain, John Earle, once gave me a big compliment when he said, "Every second is accounted for at your practices. They are fast-paced, intense and efficient. I love watching practices. The guys are getting after it the whole time."

An assistant coach at Navy, Mick Yokitis, was visiting practice at Plano East one day and said, "I could watch your practice all day. I love the tempo and pace your guys practice with. They are moving 100 mph and it's impressive."

With proper planning, practices can be fast and productive. I'm not sure why anyone would do it any other way.

THERE IS ENERGY IN MUSIC

We believe in music at practice. Research on the effects of music during exercise has been done for years. In 1911, Leonard Ayres found cyclists pedaled faster while listening to music, than they did in silence.

This happens because listening to music can drown out our brain's cries of fatigue. As our body realizes we're tired and wants to stop, it sends signals to the brain to stop for a break. Listening to music competes for our brain's attention and can help us override those signals of fatigue, though this is mostly beneficial for low- and moderate-intensity exercise.

During high-intensity exercise, music isn't as powerful at pulling our brain's attention away from the pain of the workout.

Not only can we push through the pain to exercise longer and harder when we listen to music, but it can actually help us to use our energy more efficiently. A 2012 study showed cyclists who listened to music required 7% less oxygen to do the same work as those who cycled in silence.

In 2007, a runner was preparing to run the Marine Corps Marathon. USA Track & Field, the national governing body for distance racing, had just decided to ban athletes from using portable music players in order "to ensure safety and to prevent runners from having a competitive edge."

The runner resolved to hide his iPod shuffle under his shirt. Many fellow runners protested the new rule, which remains in effect today in an amended form: It now applies only to people vying for awards and money.

In a 2012 review of the research, Costas Karageorghis of Brunel University in London, one of the world's leading experts on the psychology of exercise music, wrote that one could think of music as "a type of legal performance-enhancing drug."

Music not only energizes us physically, but mentally as well. Research has shown that it stimulates our brain and helps with learning. When applied to the context of athletics, it's very interesting to consider.

Education Professor Mary Ann Davies of Northern Arizona wrote an article in 2000 titled, "Learning ... The Beat Goes On."

Professor Davies found that music aids with memory recollection. "The hemispheres of your brain work together when emotions are stimulated, attention focused and motivation heightened. Rhythm acts as a hook for capturing attention and stimulating interest. Once a person is motivated and actively involved, learning is optimized.

The word "rhythm" here is significant, because not only is rhythm important to music, it's also what a football team seeks to establish on the field." Bottom line: Music helps the brain connect when learning and establish a rhythm in learning.

"Music captures our attention and balances repetition with novelty, which in turn, facilities retention. Additionally, our bodies 'feel' the rhythm. The rhythm, the beat, aids our physical sense in the remembering process," added Davies.

Music ... it does a body good both physically and mentally.

TAKES ENERGY TO GIVE ENERGY

You can't give what you don't have. To have energy you must be in shape and be able to coach hard for 2+ hours. I hate to say it, but you can't be overweight and coach with a ton of energy.

Brian Cain told me the first time we met last year, "Leaders aren't fat. Coach, you aren't fat, but you are getting there."

Ouch. He was 100% correct. I was getting there. I weighed 260 pounds and hadn't worked out in years.

Brian added, "Think about all the head coaches and assistant coaches you see on the sidelines of games on television. They look like they are in shape and could still play. The first step in becoming a leader is taking care of yourself and getting in shape.

I know this is easier said than done. If you can find 30

minutes a day to exercise it will make a big difference. To be your best you must look and feel your best. For years I didn't care if I looked like a leader or had the energy to 'bring it' everyday, but I can honestly say I am a better coach because I am in better shape physically. Find the time to make this a priority and you will never go back to being an out-of-shape coach.

CHAPTER 4 REVIEW
LESSON #1 ENERGY AND TEMPO

☐ Bettger changed his career by changing one thing ... his level of enthusiasm.

☐ Leaders set the example. The head coach and assistant coaches must model high energy and enthusiasm.

☐ 5:1 is the magic ratio of positive to negative.

☐ Energy must be consistent. Great coaches give feedback every play.

☐ Speed rules. When in doubt ... ATTACK!

☐ There is science behind the positive effects of music. Use it to help create energy and aid in the learning process in your workouts.

☐ Leaders aren't fat. To be a high-energy coach you must be your best physically. Find the time to be the best you possibly can!

CHAPTER 5

LESSON #2 – COMPETE

"Always compete. It's truly that simple. Find a way to do your best. Compete in everything you do."

Pete Carroll
Head Coach
Seattle Seahawks

Magic Johnson and Larry Bird faced off against each other in 1979 when Michigan State defeated Indiana State in one of the most memorable NCAA Championship games of all time.

Johnson's Spartans won the game and both entered the NBA the following season. For the next 13 years they battled each other fiercely, and met three times in the NBA Finals. The Lakers won twice and the Celtics once. Magic and Bird are two of the top players to ever play the game of basketball.

"When the new schedule would come out each year," Magic says, "I'd grab it and circle the Boston games. To me it was 'The Two' and the other 80."

"The first thing I would do every morning was look at the box scores to see what Magic did," said Bird. "I didn't care about anything else."

At his retirement speech, Johnson spoke about the

impact Bird had on his career.

"Larry was the only player in the league that I feared and the smartest player I ever played against," Johnson said. "I always enjoyed competing against him because he brought out the best in me. Even when we weren't going head to head, I would follow his game because I always used his play as a measuring stick against mine. Without Larry Bird, there would be no Magic Johnson."

COMPETITION MAKES US BETTER

Competition brings out the best in us. Magic Johnson worked years mastering his craft, yet he credits Larry Bird with helping him fulfill

PEOPLE NEVER REACH THEIR BEST WITHOUT OTHERS.

his potential to become a Top 50 player of all time.

There are countless examples of rivals who credit the other for helping them become their best. Phil Mickelson speaks of the effect of playing in the same era as Tiger Woods.

"In the last five or six years, I've had some pretty good success head-to-head and I feel like he brings out the best golfer in me. He's a great motivator for me. He's helped me work hard. He's helped me put forth the effort to try to compete at the highest-level year-in and year-out, and I've loved competing against him. He's really brought out the best in me, especially when we are paired together."

Babe Ruth hit 60 home runs in 1927. The record had stood for 34 years when teammates Mickey Mantle and Roger Maris of the Yankees started hitting homers at a pace that began to threaten the most popular record in all of sports at the time.

They battled each other every day throughout the summer of 1961. Not only were they teammates, Maris batted third and Mantle, cleanup. The home run lead would change numerous times throughout the summer.

Maris would eventually break the record with his 61st home run on the final day of the season. Both said later the competition between them was key to Maris breaking the record and Mantle hitting 54 homers before an injury sidelined him in September.

COMPETITION IS A STRUGGLE TO DEFEAT ANOTHER

Merriam Webster says competition is "the process of trying to win something (such as a prize) that someone else is also trying to win." Another description says competition is a struggle between two groups to obtain something in limited supply.

When most people think of competition, it's to defeat another person or team. The Latin root for compete means striving together (com-pete) with others to improve. To compete is to measure you against something for achievement. The more you do this the more your performance has a chance to improve.

World records are broken at track meets and swim meets. Athletes need the competition from other athletes to force them to run or swim their best times. Practice prepares them for the meet. Their coaches are making sure they are training to "peak" on that certain date, but the element of competition is essential to world records being broken.

Michael Johnson broke the world record in both the 200 and the 400 at the 1996 Olympics in Atlanta. He ran amazing times of 19.32 and 43.49. There's no doubt his training for the past year had prepared him to be in top condition physically and mentally for the Olympics. There is also no doubt he would not have ran those times on the same date in an empty stadium at practice.

He needed competition.

He had to have other world-class runners to bring out his best. He had to have the bright lights and the spotlight to give him the little bit of anxiety to perform to his maximum potential.

We remind our guys to value good players and teams we face.

"Appreciate someone who is making you better. Tell them thank you when you face a player that brings out your best. We all want to win and dominate our opponent, but if we only face players and teams that aren't as good as we are we will not reach our potential."

In spring ball we often have the offensive linemen verbally recognize the defensive lineman that made them better that day and visa versa. The defensive backs will call out receivers who made them better that day, etc. Getting units to appreciate guys making them better allows competition to not be personal, but it makes them welcome it.

We will discuss how coaches can create a competitive culture in their program in this chapter. An environment of both 'mono a mono' and 'you vs. yesterday.'

Both forms of competition are vital to teams who overachieve.

> *"I've been up against tough competition my whole life. I wouldn't know how to get along without it."*
> **Walt Disney**

COMPETITION MUST OCCUR DAILY

As I just stated, game competition is the very best form of competition. The only problem with this is we can't wait until game day to compete. Our players (and yours) probably don't have to compete a ton in other areas of their life. We must condition them to compete daily.

Being 'in the arena' shouldn't be an unusual thing. Our athletes do it everyday.

One of my biggest thrills as a coach was recently getting

to sit down with Kansas State head coach Bill Snyder. Coach Snyder was inducted into the 2015 College Football Hall of Fame and is arguably a Top 10 coach in the history of college football.

What can't be argued is his impact on the university and the town of Manhattan. He is a legend. Manhattan is the town that Bill Snyder built. After we sat down and introduced ourselves, Coach Snyder asked, "Randy, what can I do to help you?"

He's a humble superstar. I've always noticed how gracious he is after games. If the cameras stay on him you can see him talking at length to the opposing head coach and players from the other team. He was just as gracious during my day there.

We talked about many topics pertaining to culture. One of the questions I asked was how they develop a competitive nature within the program.

"Make them compete in every drill possible and make sure there are consequences for both sides. We keep score in individual, group and team drills." We vary the rewards and punishments, but two examples would be: winners have less end-of-practice running. Losing units will have 'up-downs' when the drill is completed. I believe this is something you must find a way to do in practice on a regular basis."

We've been keeping score during practice for a couple of seasons in Grapevine. We started doing it after I read Pete Carroll's outstanding book.

Coach Carroll talks about the importance of competition

throughout the book. He also discusses keeping score of drills during group and team sessions.

We borrowed some of his ideas when we set up our parameters for our scoring systems, but also made our scoring system fit for us. You may have to tweak it to fit your system. It's imperative your scoring system does not lean toward either side of the ball.

Examples of how we keep score at practice:

PASS SKELETON (7 v. 7)
- Completion by the offense = +1 for offense
- Incompletion = +1 for defense
- Interception = +3 for defense

TEAM (11 v. 11)
- 1st Down
  Offense gains +4 yards or more = +1 for offense
  3 yards or less on first down = +1 for defense

- 2nd Down
  Offense gains ½ yards needed for 1st down = +1 for offense

  If yardage gained less than ½ needed for 1st down = +1 for defense

- 3rd or 4th Down
  If offense makes a first down = +1 for offense
  First down not converted = +1 for defense

- Big play
  +15 yards by offense = +2 for offense

· Turnover
  Created by defense = +3 for defense

EARN IT

'Earn everything everyday' is one of our common phrases at Grapevine. Competition is what forces us to earn what we want.

When our guys arrive each day they know they are going to compete. We will force them be their best and hold them accountable against their past performances.

We will also call guys out to compete '1 v. 1' in front of the entire team. This is very powerful. It brings out their best. It's the closest thing to a 'fist fight' our guys get in.

Examples of how we have our guys compete each day are:

CIRCLE OF LIFE - The team circles up around mid-field during the season or the wrestling mat out of season. We call two guys out. They come to the middle (enthusiastically) and square off vs. each other. In season both get in a normal three-point stance very close to  each other (about 6"). When the whistle blows each player attacks the other.

The objective is for one to put the other "on skates." When we are not in season the two wrestle until one is pinned. Both are intense, physical battles in front of their teammates.

Examples of drills we use to have our players compete in season:

'MATCH DRILL' — A 1-on-1 drill with wide receivers competing against defensive backs. A coach points at one of the cones we have set out. The cone indicates to the receiver the correct pass route to run. The defensive back attempts to cover him. There is no tackling in this drill, but all know it is pass and there are only a few different routes that can be ran so our defensive backs can be very aggressive. Both offensive and defensive players must compete to be successful.

'BALL DOWN' — Early in practice we do an 11 v. 11 team session that is 'live.. We tackle to the ground. Each day the situation is different.

- Monday - goal line
- Tuesday - third down and long
- Wednesday - 2 minute drill or overtime

'Ball down' serves two purposes: we work a critical situation each day, but it also forces our guys to have their intensity high at the beginning of practice. We have them compete early to set the tone for the remainder of practice.

> *"Work like there is someone working twenty-four hours a day to take it all away from you."*
>
> **Mark Cuban**
> **Dallas Mavericks**

WHAT IS MEASURED IMPROVES

I call this is the 'fitbit phenomenon.' I asked for one last Christmas so I could track my workouts. After wearing mine a few weeks I realized if our entire team had a fitbit or a measuring device they would push even harder.

Not only would our guys be able to see their results, but we would also get the data (and post it everyday, of course).

Just recently I discovered and began working out at a place called Orange Theory. At Orange Theory you wear a heart rate monitor. I wear one across my chest. It's not as comfortable as a wrist monitor, but it's more accurate and I want to know exactly how hard my heart is working and how many calories I'm burning. It motivates me.

POST DAILY ACCOMPLISHMENT AND YOUR ATHLETES WILL STRIVE TO MOVE UP THE LIST.

At Orange Theory they have big monitors in the room that display everyone's calories burned, heart rate and how many minutes your heart rate has been in the 'orange zone.'

This is probably just the coach in me, but I not only

check my progress during the workout, I also check out the data from the other people working out. I'm competing against people I don't know, but the information is there and I want to keep up or exceed what they are doing. It drives me to be my best. There is no way the lady with the head band on is going to have more minutes in the orange zone than me!!!

At the university level, bar speed and power are being measured during weight lifting. On our visit to Kansas State we were given a tour of the weight room.

When I saw a tablet in the top right hand corner of the weight rack I had to ask what it was about. The tablet has the workout for the day programmed for each lifter.

Not only does it display the workout, it displays the bar speed and power generated. Like Orange Theory, there are large monitors hanging on the wall to display the results. I love it.

CREATE SCHOOL RECORDS IN EVERYTHING POSSIBLE

This is a way for athletes to compete in a realm they couldn't do in the past. I can imagine two athletes lifting at different racks and competing to see who can generate the most power as they are squatting or doing power cleans.

In 2015, Jim Harbaugh was hired to get Michigan football back to national prominence. They were outstanding in his first year going 10-3. Competition and toughness are two things he mentions a lot when describing what the Wolverines emphasize in their program.

Last season there were 105 players on the roster. They have roughly 85 scholarship players and 20 walk-on players. At the end of practice the coaches break down the film like staffs at all colleges and many high schools do, but what they do differently is each day they rank each player and post for all to see.

They measure the performance of every player, each day at practice. This would be a great motivator for me if I were playing for Michigan. I would grind even more each day to move up the list.

Knowing my performance was going to be ranked would drive me to compete against my fellow teammates and compete against myself. I would want up that list!!

Art Briles, the former coach at Baylor, has always been an amazingly successful football coach. His high school teams won multiple state championships in Stephenville, Texas.

When he got his chance to run the programs at Houston and Baylor, both won at levels higher than they had in several years (or ever).

At Stephenville High School, the football team had school records on the normal things like bench press, squat, power cleans, 40-yard dash, etc.

They also had school records for things that are not common. Certain mat drills were recorded and posted. How fast they could get through the 'monkey bars.'

Anything and everything they could make competitive they did through measuring and ranking their athletes.

Everything that can be measured can be improved. Track everything and make everything competitive.

IT PAYS TO BE A WINNER

In real life everyone doesn't really get a trophy. One of the definitions of competition is that two groups are straining to acquire something that is in limited supply. Have your team compete as much as possible every day and have it "not be ok" to lose.

The University of Houston football program had a tremendous turnaround in 2015. I attended two spring practices prior to the season in March of that year and it was apparent from the beginning the Cougars were going to be a team that would compete very hard.

Everything was important. My biggest 'take home' was the intensity of practice and the competition element. Guys were competing in every play and every drill.

During practice I began visiting with Tony Heath, head coach at Pearland High School. He said the standard was set in their offseason conditioning sessions in January.

"January workouts were the most intense I have ever seen," he said. "The competition and toughness was partially instilled in their offseason workouts."

I asked offensive line coach, Derek Wareheim, what the number one thing they were focusing on to change the culture. "Constant competition; reward winners and punish losers. Remind them how awful it is to lose. Everyone trains for war, but we train for chaos."

One example Coach Wareheim gave me was their offseason competition 'Olympics.' Most programs do this. Olympics are weekly competitions. Captains and or coaches draft teams. Point totals are kept for the duration of the Olympics. Most programs will compete weekly for 4-6 weeks.

At Houston, when the Olympics were complete, the winners were rewarded and the losers didn't fare so well. The winners ate steak and the losers ... hot dogs.

Coach Snyder mentioned consequences to me when we spoke about the value of competition. Coach Harbaugh and his staff are making it a daily aspect of their practices for every one of their 105 players and it is a vital component to the process for Coach Herman at Houston.

I could go on and on mentioning examples of this, but the bottom line is as a coach you must go the extra mile and make sure it pays to be a winner and isn't fun to be a loser.

THEY HAVE TO EARN THEIR SPOT IN THE LOCKER ROOM

When we start offseason each year, we move all our guys into the JV locker room. We give them a plain, white t-shirt with a big red "?" on the front. It means 'we don't know about you.'

They have to prove themselves to us each year.

We also take a permanent marker and write their name and lift maxes on the back of the shirt. We put their 400-meter and 40-yard dash time on the front.

After eight weeks, we begin giving them the opportunity to move into the varsity locker room. When this happens they also get much nicer gear to wear. They have to win their way into the locker room.

We have our guys vote on who comes over first. He goes into locker #1. This past year we had them vote on who was the most dependable person on the team. A couple of days later he and I discussed which player should be given the chance to move into locker #2.

HAVE YOUR PLAYERS PROVE THEMSELVES THROUGH COMPETITION.

We decided on two guys. They competed in the 'Circle of Life' by wrestling. It was a battle!! They know if they don't win it could be a couple of weeks before they get the opportunity again.

I will discuss our boot camp we do each February in depth in Chapter 8, but it's a competition that takes almost three weeks. Boot camp is one of the best things we do to establish our standard of discipline. At the end, the winning platoon is served breakfast tacos and drinks by the two losing platoons. After our spring game, the winning team gets hamburgers and the losing team gets hot dogs (I tell them how hot dogs are made so they totally understand the consequences of losing).

Our guys don't complain about these things because they understand it is our standard. "Sprinkles are for winners!" — Flo (Geico Insurance commercial)

IMPROVEMENT IS ALSO A MAJOR BENEFIT OF COMPETITION

In athletics it pays to win, but winning is something you cannot control. None of us have any control over our opponent. At Grapevine, we will always reward our winners and punish our losers, but we stress to them the way to win is to make sure you control what you can control.

Being the best YOU possible.

> "Nothing worth having comes easy."
>
> **Theodore Roosevelt**

Ashley Merryman is a scientist who has studied the science of competition. "The benefit of competition isn't the win," Merryman said. "The benefit of competition is improvement ... it's improvement in the moment."

Coach Carroll echoes Merryman's views.

"Competition is not about beating your opponent. It's about doing your best; it's about striving to reach your potential; and it's being in the relentless pursuit of a competitive edge in everything you do."

In our varsity locker room we have a large mannequin we call 'Next.' It's a faceless mannequin dressed in all white and gray gear.

'Next' wears a white helmet with no logos on it, a gray jersey with no numbers and plain white pants. There's nothing special about him. There isn't supposed to be.

He represents our next opponent and we don't treat them as special. We worry about us. If we control what we can control — our preparation and our performance — we feel good about our chances.

Worry about your team much more than your opponent. It's 'You vs. Yesterday' and getting 1% better each day.

SPUTNIK GOT US IN THE SPACE RACE

"Son, come with me out to the front porch. Look in the sky, what do you see?" The year was 1957 and Dr. Rob Gilbert was a nine-year-old boy growing up in Boston, Massachusetts. "I see stars, dad."

"No, look closer. Look over there."

"Oh, yes I see an airplane. I see it flying right over there." "No son that is not an airplane. That is a Soviet satellite named Sputnik."

That launch ushered in a competition between the U.S. and the U.S.S.R. It marked the beginning of the Space Age and the race to control outer space. With it brought new political, military, technological and scientific developments.

The Sputnik launch changed everything. As a technical achievement, Sputnik caught the world's attention and the American public off-guard.

We believed the Soviets ability to launch satellites also translated into the capability to launch ballistic missiles that could carry nuclear weapons from Europe to the U.S.

As Dr. Gilbert was telling me this story he said, "It scared America. We all believed whoever landed on the moon first would control outer space and eventually rule the world."

We got into high gear. President Kennedy made a bold proclamation to the world when he said we would land a man on the moon and safely return him by the end of the decade. When he was assassinated in 1961, we went into overdrive.

On July 20, 1969, Buzz Armstrong stepped onto the surface of the moon and we had beaten the Soviets. We had accomplished the mission.

"Everyone was unified to make it happen," said Dr. Gilbert. "Once a reporter was visiting NASA in Houston and asked a custodian what his job was and the custodian replied, 'I am helping put a man on the moon, sir.'"

Without Sputnik flying across the sky in 1957, we would not have had the 'fire in our belly' to win the space race. It takes competition from others to bring out our best.

CHAPTER 5 REVIEW
LESSON #2 COMPETE

☐ Competition makes us better. We can't reach our full potential without others pushing us to improve.

☐ Competition is a struggle against a worthy opponent. Make sure your players value others that make them better.

☐ Daily competition is vital. Make your practices as competitive as possible.

☐ What is measured improves. Post results daily and your athletes will strive to move up the list.

☐ It cannot be ok to lose. Have rewards for winners and consequences for losers.

☐ Improvement is a major benefit of competition. Reaching our potential is focusing on us and not our "next" opponent.

CHAPTER 6

LESSON #3 – TOUGHNESS

> *"Gold medals aren't really made of gold. They are made of sweat, determination, and a hard-to-find alloy called guts."*
>
> **Dan Gable**
> **Wrestler and Coach**

Dan Gable was one of the greatest wrestlers of all time. In the late 1960's, he won two national championships at Iowa State. His collegiate record stands at an amazing 118-1.

In the 1972 Olympics, Gable won the gold medal and didn't give up a single point. This was after injuring his left leg and needing seven stitches in his forehead after the first match.

One of the reason's Gable was so dominant was his work ethic. When he was wrestling at Iowa State the team practiced everyday from 4-6:30 p.m. The last 30 minutes was an insane type of conditioning.

Afterwards, all but Gable would go eat once they drug themselves into the shower and slowly exited the facility. Gable instead would go back to his locker and put on a rubber suit and then go back to the wrestling room.

While his teammates could barely walk to the cafeteria for dinner Gable would jump rope like a man possessed. His goal was to jump rope until he passed out. He never did it. As hard as he tried, he never passed out.

He was an even better coach than a wrestler. In 1976, Gable was hired by the University of Iowa to be their head wrestling coach. They wouldn't regret it.

Gable is the most successful collegiate wrestling coach in history. His teams won 15 NCAA championships during his time there, including a record nine in a row from 1978-1986. Sports Illustrated called Dan Gable the Sports Figure of the Century, but even with all these accomplishments he could not achieve what his daughter did while running track.

The Gable's had four daughters. Molly Gable was an 800-meter runner in high school. She had never qualified for the state meet and it was her senior year. She desperately wanted to qualify. To advance to the state meet Molly would have to defeat the defending state champion.

Gable was the U.S. Olympic coach and was called to Colorado for an emergency meeting and was not able to be at the meet, but his wife would be giving him 'play-by-play' via cell phone during the race.

He told Molly to stay with her and "draft" behind her. Molly did exactly this and was running great the first two laps. After the third lap, she was right behind the state champion. With 200 meters to go, Molly passed her and took the lead. She was still barely in the lead down the home stretch. Molly was on the verge of a massive upset victory!

Mrs. Gable was going crazy calling the action for him and then all of the sudden she goes silent ... for what seemed like an eternity to Gable. Then she says, "Dan, she fell and had to crawl across the finish line."

He caught the first plane back to Iowa and sped home. Molly was devastated. She was in her bedroom and had cried so much her pillow was soaked.

Gable asked her to tell him what happened. Molly said, "I did exactly what you said. I was pushing myself harder than I ever have before. I was right with her. Then, everything went blank. I think I passed out."

Gable told this story during one of his many speeches. He told it with great pride in his heart and tears in his eyes. "My daughter did what I could never do. She pushed herself to collapse."

MENTAL AND PHYSICAL TOUGHNESS

WILLPOWER – being able to control yourself.

GRIT – strength of mind to be able to endure pain and hardship.

In materials science and metallurgy, toughness is the ability of a material to absorb energy and plastically deform without fracturing. It's also defined as a material's resistance to fracturing when stressed.

Scientists can measure how tough a material is by integrating the 'stress strain curve.' They use terms like 'units of toughness.' We don't have a formula to measure how tough humans are, but we do have terms to describe toughness also. Grit and willpower are my two favorites.

COMFORTABLE BEING UNCOMFORTABLE

There are lots of great definitions for toughness. Ours is borrowed from the Navy Seals; 'Comfortable being Uncomfortable.'

We are going to have our guys uncomfortable.

Growth only occurs when the body is stretched beyond its normal capacity. The body gets accustomed to being stretched. When it's stretched on a regular basis, improvement occurs and it can be stretched a little more.

Mental toughness is toughness. All toughness must be developed in the mind. We talk about both in our core values, but physical toughness is a byproduct of mental toughness. Toughness is at the core of our program in Grapevine and has been for all my teams since TPW became our 'brand' in 2004 at Lone Oak High School.

> *"I've never met a strong person with an easy past."*
>
> *Unknown*

Our team knows we are always striving to have our own 'culture language' and want all to be able to speak 'fluent TPW.'

There are certain words and phrases we say a lot and want our guys to use. One of the phrases we say is 'alpha male.'

MENTALLY TOUGH PEOPLE WIN. THE MIND OF A CHAMPION DEALS WITH CHALLENGES AND DOESN'T GIVE IN TO THEM.

We want alpha males. An alpha male is the dominant male in the group. He's confident and tough. I'm not sure you can make alpha males out of just anyone, but I do know you can bring it out of guys who have some toughness.

GRIT IS THE #1 FACTOR IN OVERACHIEVING

Angela Duckworth is a scientist who studies achievement, specifically how mental toughness, perseverance and grit impact people's ability to achieve goals. She studied incoming cadets at West Point to see what differentiates the ones who are able to achieve success in their very tough first year.

Duckworth studied a total of 2,441 cadets spread across two entering classes. Their SAT scores, high school rank, extracurricular activities, Physical Aptitude Exam (standardized physical exercise evaluation) and Grit Scale (measures perseverance and passion for long-term goals) were all recorded.

Intelligence was not the #1 determining factor for a cadet's success. Neither was strength or leadership potential. Instead, it was grit; the strength of mind to endure hardship or pain that made the difference.

Talent is overrated!! Grit is essential to overachieving.

SEAL GRADUATION RATES ARE 30%, MOST DROPOUT DURING THE 'DROWNING TEST'. TRAINEES STAY UNDER WATER WHILE INSTRUCTORS HARASS THEM BY TURNING OFF THEIR OXYGEN AND RIPPING OFF THEIR FACE MASK TO SIMULATE CONDITIONS CLOSE TO DROWNING.

4 COMPONENTS OF MENTAL TOUGHNESS

1. Willpower – self-control
2. Being able to bounce back after a bad play or loss.
3. Positive self-talk. Not listening to yourself, but talking to yourself.
4. Courageous – players who play with guts.

HAVING THE WILLPOWER TO HANDLE GETTING 'SUGAR-COOKIED'

Admiral William H. McRaven, former Navy Seal, gave a speech to the graduating class at the University of Texas in 2014. He spoke about some of the hardships BUD/S candidates go through. One of the things in his speech we talk about in our program is getting 'sugar cookied.'

"Several times a week, the instructors would line up the class and do a uniform inspection. It was exceptionally thorough. Your hat had to be perfectly starched, your uniform immaculately pressed and your belt buckle shiny and void of any smudges.

The 70% of SEAL CANDIDATES WHO ARE DROPOUTS DON'T GET TO SNEAK OUT IN THE MIDDLE OF THE NIGHT. THEY MUST "RING THE BELL".

But it seemed that no matter how much effort you put into starching your hat, or pressing your uniform or polishing your belt buckle, it just wasn't good enough.

The instructors would find something wrong.

"For failing the uniform inspection, the student had to run, fully-clothed into the surf zone and then, wet from head to toe, roll around on the beach until every part of your body was covered with sand. The effect was known as a 'sugar cookie.'

"You stayed in that uniform the rest of the day — cold, wet and sandy."

"There was many a student who just couldn't accept the fact that all their effort was in vain. That no matter how hard they tried to get the uniform right, it was unappreciated. Those students didn't make it through training. Those students didn't understand the purpose of the drill. You were never going to succeed. You were never going to have a perfect uniform."

"Sometimes no matter how well you prepare or how well you perform you still end up as a sugar cookie. It's just the way life is sometimes."

Stressful situations are going to happen in every game. Things we have no control over; an official will make an incorrect call, the weather will turn bad during the game, one of your best players will get injured. The list can go on and on. Your team is going to get 'sugar-cookied.' You must train them to be able to deal with it.

MENTAL TOUGHNESS IS BEING ABLE TO 'SHAKE IT OFF'

'So what, next play' is one of our mantras. One of the differences in great players and average players is their ability to get over a mistake in a hurry. 'shake it off,' forget about it and compete on the next play. One of the best descriptions of mental toughness I have heard anywhere was by Bruce Brown of Proactive Coaching.

> *"Mental toughness is how quickly an athlete can get over failure. If it takes him/her a while to 'shake it off' then they must play a sport that moves slow."*
>
> **Bruce Brown**
> **Proactive Coaching**

Holy cow, Bruce makes a lot of sense. In volleyball, when a first serve is hit just wide the server has two options mentally in the next few seconds; she can dwell on what just happened, replay the shot and decide if the official made the correct call or she can say, 'so what, next play,' shake it off and put her total focus on the next serve.

Every coach reading this knows what we hope she will do.

'HURRY UP NEXT PLAY'

I am a big believer in playing 'pedal to metal,' offensively. Most talk about it impacting defenses physically, but it also impacts them mentally.

They don't have much time to 'get over it' before we are running another play.

OUR GOALS IS TO SNAP THE BALL IN 12-15 SECONDS FROM THE END OF THE PREVIOUS PLAY. THIS IS NOT MUCH TIME FOR A DEFENSIVE PLAYER TO PREPARE OR RECOVER MENTALLY.

I first learned how to play with tempo from the Tony Franklin System in 2007 when I was the head coach in Lone Oak. A friend of mine, who coached at a larger school, suggested it to me. At first I thought we wouldn't have the depth for it. We only suited out 25 on the varsity and I didn't know if our guys could handle it, physically.

Every defensive coach reading this would be worried about the occasional 'three-and-out' and having our guys switch over to defense after only 55 seconds has run off the clock. It was a valid concern for me as well.

Playing with tempo was one of the best things I have done as a football coach. It's even better at the small school level. We didn't play 'hair on fire' every snap, but anytime we had a play of 10 yards or more you could count on us yelling 'Nascar!, Nascar!' from the sideline.

In 2007, tempo was not as common as it is now. Our opponents struggled with our pace. In the second half, sometimes our offensive linemen would signal to us to go Nascar pace. They would sense when the opposing defensive linemen would be getting very tired and were not playing with the same intensity.

When offenses huddle there is some time to exhale and everyone is allowed an extra 20-25 seconds to get their bearings before the next 'attack.'

THE TEMPO BUY-IN

In my first season at Poteet, we installed our fast-paced offense. Poteet is a much larger school and we didn't have guys playing 'both ways' (two-way players who played both offense and defense). Because we were able to two-platoon most of our guys, the issue of wearing our own guys down was no longer a factor. We began to play as fast as we could every play.

I touched on this in Chapter 1, but Poteet had struggled before 2010. One of the things you must do to change a culture is to be different from your predecessor. Our tempo was different and it was not only an advantage schematically, but mentally as well.

We started 1-0 by defeating Royse City 40-19 on the road. Our next game was with Arlington Seguin at home.

They were impressive in warm-ups. They wore black, sleeveless compression shirts with a big 'Superman S' logo on the front. I said to one of our coaches, "maybe we should leave our guys in the locker room so they won't see these beasts out here."

I was kidding, but I did wish they were wearing shoulder pads across the field.

It was hot when the game started. We told the team our tempo would wear Seguin down mentally and physically. At halftime I asked our offensive line if their defensive players were getting tired and all said yes. Our tempo was relentless. The pace affected them and we won the game 27-7.

Seguin was exhausted when it was over. With just a few minutes left one of our players said to me, "look coach, all of their guys are on the bench. You were right, we wore them out."

He was right, not one player was standing watching the game. Everyone on the sideline was sitting down.

Within the past couple of years, two high-profile college coaches, Nick Saban of Alabama and Bret Bielema of Arkansas, have spoken out on the danger of fast-tempo offenses on defensive players. They argue there is not enough recovery time, etc. (although 'Bama played some tempo in the 2016 National Championship game).

You don't hear of coaches talking about how tough tempo is on their team mentally, but I believe it is just as big a weapon for the offense. When the ball is snapped as quickly as we do, the defense does not have time to 'get over it.'

When we hit them with a big play (+15 yards or more is our definition), not only is their mind trying to figure out how to line up, but they are playing at a pace that does not give them much time to recover, physically.

BOOT CAMP IS OUR 'MENTAL MARATHON'

Great teams are made in the offseason. We accomplish a lot in quarters 1 and 2. Quarter 1 is the beginning of our offseason and we emphasize strength and power. In February, we start Quarter 2 with boot camp. If you asked our guys to list what gives us the 'edge' to a man all would have boot camp in their near the top. Most would have it #1.

Coaches have told me, "we work our guys hard everyday. We don't need a boot camp."

We work our guys really hard also and ask them to do a lot of extra in addition to our normal workouts. They wrestle, run track, power lift and more. Even with all this, boot camp is vital to our program.

Why? They have to be mentally tough to get through it and succeed. Our boot camp is a mental marathon. I am always impressed by how our guys handle it.

During boot camp, we track mistakes made by each athlete. Each day we post mistakes made daily and a cumulative total. They are drafted into three platoons and each competes to be 'boot camp champion.'

We take control from the start. They have two minutes to get dressed (in total silence) and be ready for inspection in front of their locker. Coaches are yelling if something is not perfect. Coaches with clipboards are marking a mistake for each name called.

There's a lot of mental strain involved, as much as we can put on them. Shoes must be tied, shirts must be tucked in, faces must be clean-shaven, lockers must be exactly right, etc.

Each day we have four stations: command weights, mat drills, jump rope and cone drills. Each station is 13 minutes in length. For two weeks we do the same four each day. All of the stations are physically demanding, but each one is a mental challenge as well.

Each has its own command words that must be followed. No movement is allowed without the appropriate command given by a coach.

For example: at command weights, the word to begin lifting might be "go" or "red" (they change each day or we can change during the station).

At the jump rope station "go" or "red" will be a command to hit a knee or stand at attention. Towards the end, one of our coaches said he had to expand some of his commands to two-word phrases to challenge them. He would say, "red-blue" means move. "Blue-red" means back to starting position.

We have a lot of future 'CEO types' in Grapevine. They are smart, mentally tough and do not make a lot of mistakes. We do get them at times, but it's not easy. When one of them does make a mistake, they have to show us they are not dwelling on it, have released it, and are ready for the next play.

This year each platoon had their own visual sign they used when a mistake was made. This sign was not to acknowledge a mistake was made, but it let everyone know they had 'flushed it' mentally. They had to do this quickly. Another command was going to be thrown at them as soon as possible.

One platoon decided their sign was to shake their hands at their side (what we all use now), one was wiping their shirt like they were dusting it off and one platoon clapped their hands.

This was new to us this year so it was a suggestion the first week, but it was a requirement the second week. If a player did not do his physical release a very loud "mistake, Smith!" would be heard.

Back when I played high school basketball you had to raise your hand when you committed a foul. If I were coaching basketball and this was still a rule (at least in Texas it is not) I would find a way to incorporate the raising of the hand and 'shake it off' together. Maybe a thumbs-up as the hand goes up in the air to let everyone know he/she has let it go and is ready to play great defense.

Boot camp is one way we get an edge. We will always do a boot camp, not to get our guys better physically, but to put them through it mentally. It's the best way we teach our players 'so what, next play.'

"Mental toughness is doing the right thing for the team when it's not the best thing for you."

Bill Belichick
Head Coach
New England Patriots

POSITIVE SELF-TALK

Everything happens twice; first in the mind and then on the field of competition. When things get tough, we must be intentional about talking to ourselves and not just listening to ourselves.

The Mayo Clinic defines self-talk as "the endless stream of unspoken thoughts that run through your head ... [that] can be positive or negative." Furthermore, "if your thoughts are mostly positive, you're likely an optimist – someone who

PEOPLE WHO OVERACHIEVE AT BOOT CAMP, SEAL TRAINING OR ANYTHING TOUGH HAVE A MINDSET TO COMPETE; THEY ARE NOT MERELY FOCUSED ON SURVIVAL.

practices positive thinking."

As the practice week goes on, it's smart to become more and more positive with your team to help them with their positive self-talk.

Del Van Cox, head football coach at Abilene High School, told me they have 'positive Wednesdays' each week to emphasize staying positive with their team.

Negative thinking can cause anyone big problems, but especially to athletes before a competition. Negative self-talk is among the biggest contributors to performance anxiety and pregame jitters.

The Mayo clinic says, "Don't say anything to yourself you wouldn't say to someone else."

We must do our part to not contribute to negative self-talk by our athletes. Early in my career I coached at Greenville High School under head coach Marvin Sedberry. He told our staff not to ever 'rip into' our players during a game.

"Build them up. They are all we have and they need to believe in themselves. If you have to fuss at them, do it on Saturday morning in film study."

We were not very good at the time, but Coach Sedberry was 100% correct. The only thing worse than not being very talented is for your not-so-talented players to not believe in themselves.

I have not always been disciplined and followed this advice, but it is exactly right. I'm thinking of getting coaching shirts to wear on Wednesdays or Thursdays next season with a large yellow smiley face on the back to reinforce positivity.

STRATEGIES TO IMPROVE SELF-TALK

1. Short term goals - Going back to SEAL BUD/S training, scientist have concluded the soldiers who focused only on the task at hand fared much better than those who didn't. In 'hell week' for instance, all of them know they have hours and hours of tough training to endure. The guys who tell themselves, "I'm not quitting before breakfast. If I can just make to breakfast" have a mental advantage over the guys who wonder how they are going to survive the next 18 hours.

Terry Fox is one of the biggest heroes in the history of Canada. ESPN even did a '30 for 30' titled "Against the Wind" in 2010.

Terry was diagnosed with bone cancer at age 18. His right leg had to be amputated right above the knee. Terry became frustrated by the lack of treatment, research and overall awareness of his form of cancer. Three years after his diagnosis, he decided to run 30 miles a day to raise funds for cancer research and awareness about the disease.

Terry decided to run from East to West, against the brutal Canadian wind blowing from West to East. His route was from Newfoundland to British Columbia. He called it the 'Marathon of Hope.'

On one leg, Terry was attempting to run over 4,000 miles, all of it against the wind.

> *"A marathon is not twenty-six miles. It is one mile twenty-six times."*
>
> **Brian Cain**
> **Peak Performance Coach**

He was a 'rock star' in Canada as the news spread about his journey. People were amazed anyone could run 30 miles a day, everyday with a prosthetic leg. When he was asked how he kept going as exhaustion set in and he had thousands of miles still ahead of him, he replied, "I just keep running to the next telephone pole."

Two-thirds across Canada Terry's cancer returned, this time it spread to his lungs. Terry had to end his Marathon of Hope. He died a few months later. He had run for 143 days and covered 3,339 miles. His amazing marathon had captured the attention of not only Canada, but the world.

Terry's self-talk was the reason he stated he was able to do it everyday. He just ran to the next telephone pole.

2. Watch their individual highlight video before each game – Have your players make a highlight video of themselves and add to it each week. Part of their pregame routine should be for them to watch it. This will give them positive affirmation before they take the field. Pete Carroll once had a highlight made for each of his

Seahawks players that was only from when they played in college.

"Football is supposed to be fun. Watch this and remember how much fun we can have when we play Arizona tomorrow," said Carroll.

3. Control breathing – Anxiety or jitters can also be reduced by increasing oxygen to the brain. I would be lying if I said we've coached breathing in Grapevine, but it is the next step we will take in our mental game approach. A simple 4 x 2 x 6 breathing exercise is a great pregame routine we will have in place this coming season. Have your athletes breathe in for 4 seconds, hold for 2 seconds and exhale for 6 seconds.

We will also train our guys to take a deep breath between plays. It will be another trigger to remind them the last play is over and get ready for the next play. I can see it working very well with our receivers. As they are getting aligned and see the signal from their coach, they will take a deep breath. Oxygen is the cure for anxiety and stress.

Muhammad Ali was ahead of his time in positive self-talk. Many of his quotes are spot-on what is being taught today. When he said 'Float like a butterfly and sting like a bee' he was not only saying it to others, he was saying it to himself. I'm sure between he and his trainer, Angelo Dundee, he heard it a thousands of times. Each time he was programming his brain to make his body 'float' and to make his punches more powerful.

'HURT - PAIN - AGONY'

James Counsilman was an Olympic swimmer and Hall of Fame swimming coach. He is best known for being the head swimming coach at Indiana University from 1957 to 1990. He was also the head coach for our Olympic swim teams for the 1964 and 1976 games.

Coach Counsilman was inducted as an Honors Coach into the International Swimming Hall of Fame in 1976. He understood his athletes had to be tough. Every year at the first practice he had the same talk with his swimmers.

- "If you want to be good and swim for IU -**Hurt** everyday at practice."

- "If you want to be a national champion - go hard enough to have **Pain** everyday at practice."

- "If you want to be a world champion - go hard enough to experience **Agony** everyday at practice."

After practice you will all feel the same. What are you willing to feel in practice?

COURAGE IS A BYPRODUCT OF TOUGHNESS

"That team played with guts."

Every coach wants this said about his or her team.

"Give me the ball, coach I want the shot. I can do it."

We also want players who aren't afraid to take the game-winning shot.

> *"Listen, we give you scholarships, we give you stipends and meals and a place to live. We give you nice uniforms. I can't give you guts! I can't give you heart and tonight it was BYOG. Bring Your Own Guts!*
>
> **Dabo Swinney**
> **Head Football Coach**
> **Clemson Tigers**

How do we develop this type of mental toughness in our team? The more mentally tough your players are the more they will have the 'guts' to perform in crunch time.

One way is to create an environment of 'winners and learners.' It pays to be a winner. I discussed it in Lesson #2, but make sure your players know when they do lose they don't lose the lesson.

As coaches, when we lose a game, we can't lose our minds. We should treat it like a medical examiner treats a dead body (I know this is a strange analogy), we examine what caused us to lose and work to fix it.

Carol Dweck is a Stanford psychologist. According to Dweck, gritty people contend with failure by implementing a 'growth mindset.' Not only has she found that the most successful people in their field have an uncanny ability to overcome adversity, but they usually stumbled their way to greatness.

> *"A setback is a setup for a comeback!"*
>
> **Reverend T.D. Jakes**

They didn't see a setback as the end of the world. They saw it as an opportunity for growth and as an inevitable part of the journey. They know that the seeds of their coming successes are planted in their setbacks.

Make sure your athletes keep the 1% warrior mentality and do not expect to master their craft in the first few days, weeks or months.

I heard a story on a podcast recently about a baseball coach working with a young player and teaching him a different way to swing the bat. After THREE SWINGS the player looked at the coach and said, "its just not working, coach. This new way will never work for me."

If we do not preach the message of continued improvement over time, the majority of our players will not grasp it. There are a million examples of great achievers who did not start great (Thomas Edison, Michael Jordan, etc.). Share these with your team and reinforce the process.

OUR SUPERMAN - BEAU NOWELL

Anyone who watched any of our playoffs in 2010 knows who Beau Nowell is.

Beau was our quarterback and he was a C.T.G. (certified tough guy). Beau wasn't going to play football his senior year. It was my first season at Poteet and I knew we needed him. When he and his dad, Ted, showed up in June to talk about playing, I was happy to see them.

Just having Beau on the team changed everything. Our trainer, Jana Foster, said to me, "Kate says we have a chance now." Kate is Jana's daughter and she was also a senior. If Kate believed Beau would make a big difference then the rest of players would also.
Kate was right. Beau was the real deal. He wasn't a big time recruit. He was a really good high school quarterback who had the biggest "it" factor of anyone I have had the pleasure to coach.

Although predicted to finish last in our district, we finished with an 8-2 regular season record and were district co-champions. We were a team of destiny. We got better each week. Our defense was very good, our kicking game was solid and we had playmakers on offense.

> *"Toughness has nothing to do with size, physical strength or athleticism. Toughness is a skill that can be developed and improved."*
>
> **Jay Bilas**
> **Basketball analyst - ESPN**

We had a lot of momentum going into our bi-district game with the Hutto Hippos. They were also 8-2 and a formidable opponent. We met them on a Saturday afternoon at a neutral site in Waco.

Midway Stadium holds 10,250 and every seat was taken. I had been a head coach only in the smaller classifications so this was something I had not experienced before.

The score was still 0-0 in the second quarter. Beau was hit like a ton of bricks by a blitzing linebacker. It happened on the Hutto side of the field and everyone of their fans were on their feet screaming.
Even as my star quarterback was on the ground I thought, "wow, that is an amazing site over there. This is big school playoffs."

We called timeout and got Beau to the sidelines. He was hurting and having a tough time breathing. He had the wind knocked out of him.

Beau didn't miss a play.

Although we did not play our best game that day, Beau played fine and we advanced 21-20.

The next week we were 14-point underdogs as we traveled to Corsicana to play the Whitehouse Wildcats. They were loaded.

Their top player was the all-time leading receiver in the state of Texas with 259 career receptions (we 'held' him to only 13). They were very good on defense also so we definitely had our hands full.

Our defense played amazing that day, but it was tough sledding on offense. It was again scoreless in the second quarter when Beau got 'rocked' again. It was like a replay from the week before. Again, Beau was lying on the turf near their sideline and again at least 5,000 Wildcat fans were going crazy.

This time I didn't think anything, but 'oh crap.' He seemed to be lying there longer and more motionless.

We called timeout again. Beau was again in pain and having a hard time catching his breath. There were about two minutes before the half when Taylor Morris, one of our offensive coaches, asked me if we wanted to put in our backup quarterback to give Beau the entire halftime to get to feeling better. I asked Beau if he was ok.

"I'm fine, coach."

"Beau's fine. Let's take a shot and see if we can get something going," was my response to Coach Morris and the rest of the offense standing around us.

We did take a shot and Beau completed a long pass to our running back, Steven Hicks, out of the backfield. Steven made it to the seven-yard line before being tackled. Our drive stalled, but we kicked the field goal and went up at half 3-0.

The final was 24-19 'good guys.'   Our defense was spectacular. The best team didn't win that day, but the team that played the best did. Although the margin was five points I will always believe Beau staying in the game before halftime was the turning point.

Momentum is a big deal. Our team seeing Beau go back onto the field and us scoring right before the half made a big statement that we would find a way.

We defeated Highland Park 45-28 in the third round, breaking an 0-14 streak against them at AT&T Stadium. In the fourth round we held on to take out Bastrop 42-35 to continue our amazing run.

This matched us up with the defending state champion Aledo Bearcats in round five.

We played at Mansfield's Newsome Stadium. Capacity is 12,000, but there were at least 13-14,000 people all in all at the game. It was even televised in the Dallas-Fort Worth Metroplex.

We had went from an afterthought in August to the surprise team of the state in December. Aledo would be the best team we played the entire year. Jonathan Gray, one of the most prolific running backs in Texas high school football history, was one of their many 'dudes.'

We were big underdogs vs. Aledo, as we should have been, but we were hanging in there.

The score was tied 7-7 in the second quarter when Beau was hit on a sprint out pass. For the third time in the playoffs he was laying on the turf. This time he was holding his leg and in obvious pain.

You have to be kidding me.

There were four minutes until halftime as the doctors took Beau in to examine his leg.

I was told at the beginning of halftime it was a broken fibula. I didn't have time to go find Beau and console him. I spent every second getting our starting receiver/backup quarterback, Courtland Crumby, ready to play the final two quarters.

Later the coaching staff told me, Beau was spending his time convincing our middle school coaches that he would indeed play in the second half.

We warmed up for the second half and Beau was still in the locker room. I don't spend time thinking 'what if'. I don't have that mindset. I wasn't wondering if Beau could possibly play. I was wondering how we could stay in the game in the second half with our game plan changing more than a little bit.

Right before the second half kickoff I heard our side of the stadium get very loud. It was like Elvis had entered the building. It might as well have been. Beau was jogging/limping over to me.

"I'm good coach. I'll be fine. Let me go to work."

I knew he couldn't play, but I also knew he was our only chance.

"Ok, you can have one series to prove to me you can go. If you can't move I'm going to take you out."

I later joked that if Beau had been in a wheelchair and wanted to play I would've told him the same thing as I pushed him out to the ball.

Beau was special. Just like Kate knew in June, Beau gave us a chance. He led us on three touchdown drives in the second half. He even limped into the end zone on a 9-yard run to tie the game at 14-14. An 11-yard touchdown pass to Crumby (who should have been playing quarterback) gave us the lead 21-14.

Beau threw his last touchdown pass to Paul Kamanda with 1:37 left in the game to pull us to within two points at 29-27. Unfortunately, our two-point conversion failed.

"It will be a performance people in Mesquite will talk

about for years," I told the Dallas Morning News.

I sure wasn't going to have a chapter about toughness and not talk about Beau Nowell, a true C.T.G.

Below is an excerpt from the Aledo News Daily following the semifinal game:

R-E-S-P-E-C-T...You Don't Tug on Superman's Cape

By Steve Keck

Something special happened during the Aledo and Poteet game. The Pirate's star quarterback suffered a broken bone in his leg. It was a clean hard hit by Aledo defensive end Slaiter Vandertuin. When I saw this happen, my immediate thought was it looked bad. The overwhelming desire in my heart was quarterback Beau Nowell would not be seriously injured.

The hit caused Nowell to be carried into the locker room. I walked by the Pirate's locker room to find out if he was okay. My job as a reporter stopped. I was genuinely concerned about the player. The press found out during halftime Nowell had suffered a broken fibula.

After the game, I asked Jackson if he was surprised to see Nowell on the sideline. "The doctors told us he had broken his fibula and would not be able to play," said Jackson. "We were having enough trouble with Beau in the game. We knew we would be in more trouble without him in the game".

Jackson had his team ready with a plan for Courtland

Crumby to play quarterback. Nowell told his coach the doctors had cleared him to play. "I gave the situation a lot of thought. I agreed to put him in for one series and see how he felt,' said Jackson. Seeing their senior leader and quarterback on the field pumped up the Pirates. Nowell played through the pain and came within an eyelash of leading Poteet into a state championship game. "That was one seriously epic effort by Beau. He is the toughest kid I have ever coached," commented Jackson.

Beau knows courage.

CHAPTER 6 REVIEW
LESSON #3 TOUGHNESS

☐ Toughness is mental toughness; it must come from the mind.

☐ Toughness is the product of struggle.

☐ Everyone gets 'sugar cookied' at times. We must respond with grit and willpower.

☐ Mental toughness is being able to shake off adversity quickly.

☐ Teams must be put in mental marathons like boot camp to test their mental toughness.

☐ Positive self-talk is a tremendous strategy to create more mental toughness. Talk to yourself, do not listen to yourself.

☐ Short term goals, personal highlight videos and controlled breathing help foster positive self-talk.

☐ There are winners and learners. Guts and courage are byproducts of loss. Gritty people understand failure is part of the process.

CHAPTER 7

LESSON #4 – FAMILY AND APPRECIATION

> *"From this day to the end of the world, be we in it shall be remembered. We few, we happy few, we band of brothers; for he today that sheds his blood with me shall be my brother."*
>
> **St. Crispen's Day Speech**
> **Shakespeare's play "Henry V"**

Henry V made the quote above (or close to it) before the Battle of Agincourt between England and France in 1415. King Henry and his 9,000 troops had been in France for months and were attempting to sail back home for the winter. The French were in pursuit with a much larger force of 36,000 men. They had cut them off from retreat and now the English, although heavily outnumbered would have to stand and fight.

Henry had to inspire his tired and weary troops to take on the advancing Frenchmen. He used two emotions to persuade his men; the glory of victory and the love of each other.

"Anyone who stays to fight will have something to boast about for the rest of his life and in the future will remember with pride the battle on this day. Every commoner who fights today with the king will become his brother. From this day to the end of the world, be we in it shall be remembered. We few, we happy few, we band of brothers; for he today that sheds his blood with me shall be my brother."

The English not only defeated the French that day, they massacred them. Their casualties were approximately 150 while the French lost between 7,000 and 10,000 men. The battle is celebrated in England still today every October 25th on St. Crispen's Day.

This speech is the first time in recorded history the phrase "Band of Brothers" was used. It is a great description of team unity that has adopted all over the world, especially since the HBO miniseries, "Band of Brothers," came out in 2001 documenting Easy Company in World War II.

Teams that are true 'Bands of Brothers' are special. They're hard to beat because they don't want to let each other down.

Like anything, if it's special it is hard to achieve. Great leaders work to build the culture of brotherhood in their organization.

F.A.M.I.L.Y - 'FORGET ABOUT ME I LOVE YOU'

Sometimes I think about what drives me as a coach. After 26 years I'm still just as excited to lead a team as I've ever been. I still love talking ball with other coaches and studying the newest trends, but as fun as it is to learn a new scheme, it's not what makes a great program.

What motivates me most is having our team play together. It's magical to see a group that is 'on a mission' together. Teamwork isn't common today. It's not easy to get teenagers (or adults for that matter) to be unselfish and play for each other.

A great program is consistent over several years. The team does not win just when it has more talent than its opponents. A consistent program finds a way to win year after year, even when there's a dip in talent.

What is one thing most have in common? They have a culture of chemistry. True success is being a part of something bigger than yourself. The team is the thing.

> *"No man is more important than the team. No coach is more important than the team. The TEAM, the TEAM, the TEAM."*
>
> **Bo Schembechler**
> **Head Football Coach**
> **University of Michigan**

Merriam Webster defines family several ways. All are relevant in a 'band of brothers' type program.

- a group of individuals living under one roof and usually under one head : household

- a group of persons of common ancestry : clan : a people or group of peoples regarded as deriving from a common stock : race

- a group of people united by certain convictions or a common affiliation

It's tougher today than ever to create a culture of TEAM. Social media fosters a 'look at me' culture. In football, early recruiting has shifted the focus for some players to 'the next level' before they are even on a varsity roster.

Recruiting services and websites promise parents help with a scholarship (side note: parents, don't spend money on recruiting services).

Some parents are more concerned with how many touches their son gets than him being a team player. I know this has always been an issue, but the early recruiting in football has only heightened it for us.

BUILDING A CULTURE OF TEAM

If you're a head coach, your most important assignment is to build a culture of team, it is also your toughest. You must, must, must work on creating an unselfish team everyday. Whatever is celebrated is repeated. A great leader celebrates those who sacrifice for the team. As a leader, do not stress only the measureables (strength, speed, talent), but focus on the intangibles. If you can get your team to play for each other because they don't want to let each other down, you will be tough to beat.

If you're an assistant coach, make sure you are doing your part also. The best companies answer questions from customers the same way no matter who answers the phone. Companies with a consistent message prosper. It's the same way with any team. The message (and standard) should be the same by each coach.

> *"The average parent spends 2.5 minutes a day in meaningful conversation with their children. They spend more time grooming themselves than raising their kids. Coaches must accept the fact they are a primary force in the life of each player."*
>
> **Gene Stallings**
> **Former Head Coach**
> **Alabama Crimson Tide and Phoenix Cardinals**

COACHES MUST BE RELATIONAL

I use the term 'kid magnet' when I'm looking to hire an assistant coach. Kid magnets are coaches who are great at relationship building, but also high energy guys. They're coaches who genuinely enjoy being around their athletes and students.

In the interview process I look for the "who" more than I do the "what." Experience and knowledge of the position is important, but they aren't the deciding factors for me.

In 2011, a player was coming back to Poteet after moving to another state. When I met with his mom, she told me her son was excited because one of his old friends told him, "you will like it, the coaches love us here now." Bam. That was music to my ears.

It isn't easy to create an environment of love from coaches to players. It takes extra time that some coaches do not want to put in. In 2012, when a coach was leaving Poteet he told our principal, "Randy is great for kids, but he is tough on assistants. He demands a lot from us as far as relationships and taking care of the players. It takes more time than other places I have coached." Yes sir, it does. Not only will we win more games because our players don't want to let us down, but it is the right thing to do. It is our responsibility as coaches.

FOLLOWERS WILL 'LAY IN TRAFFIC' FOR A GREAT LEADER

None of us hear the phrase "good job" enough. I once worked for a head coach that said, "If you need to hear good job a lot to keep you going, you will be disappointed here."

He was right. It was disappointing to grind and not get any positive feedback for your efforts. It wasn't much fun at times wondering if I was making my boss happy.

My coaches hear this from me, "if your players won't lay in traffic for you, something is wrong."

It's hard to lay in traffic for someone who doesn't celebrate your work. I learned this the hard way and discussed it in Chapter 1; **go where you are celebrated and not tolerated**. It's the same with players. We have to recruit our own players.

TELL THREE PLAYERS A DAY HOW MUCH YOU APPRECIATE AND VALUE THEM. DO THIS AFTER PRACTICE VERBALLY OR WITH A TEXT.

There are a lot of options for young people today. One of them is to do nothing. When I was growing up in Tenaha we made fun of the guys who weren't athletes (not really, but you know what I mean). Today, it is not a big deal for kids to specialize or just stay in the house and do nothing.

At Grapevine, each coach will text three players a day to tell them 'great job' during the offseason. It's an easy thing to do that makes three guys feel a little more appreciated.

Nick Saban talked about this very thing at a clinic a few years ago regarding affirming players; "I realized I was spending 98% of my time on the 2% who weren't doing things right. Now, we focus time everyday on the guys who are doing everything we ask. We need to affirm the guys who are going to class, always on time for weight workouts and meetings. Everyday after practice we all (coaches) find three guys who are 'all in' and go tell them thank you."

> *"The way you speak to your children is the single greatest factor in shaping their personalities and self-confidence."*
>
> **Brian Tracy**
> **Motivational Expert**

After practice we gather up and I ask coaches to point out players who did a great job that day. I also have the players identify guys they know who went above and beyond. They love giving one of their teammates recognition.

A lot of times we tie it in with our core value of the day. On Monday, we talk about our high-energy guys and recognize them. On Tuesday, we identify the guys who competed the hardest and so on.

BREAK BREAD AND SPEND TIME
WITH YOUR PLAYERS

Our position coaches will eat every few weeks with their position players. This is a big deal to me. If the linebackers meet up with their coach (players pay for their meal) and spend some time together it helps bond them as a unit. The coaches connect with them in a low-stress setting.

Rodney Webb is the head football coach at Rockwall High School in Rockwall, Texas and one of the best coaches in the state. He has his staff eat pregame meals with their position group each week before games. He says they can talk about anything ... except football.

This spring I started feeling guilty about asking the coaches so I decided I needed to do my part also. I started inviting 15 guys over to my house every few weeks for what I call 'Relationship Dinners.'

> *"If soldiers are punished before they have grown attached to you, they will not prove submissive."*
>
> **Sun Tzu**

Shannon makes spaghetti with all the trimmings. After they eat and visit with each other for around 45 minutes we gather in the living room. We form a semi-circle so we're all able to see each other. I have specific questions I ask each player one at a time. We go around the room and then we go to question 2 and so on.

The topics we use are:

1. Tell us about your family.

2. What is one goal you have for this spring?

3. Ten years from now what is your career goal / what type of job do you want to be doing?

4. What is your favorite memory from little league or middle school football?

5. What is your favorite core value and why?

6. What is something no one in this room knows about you?

7. What is the toughest thing you have ever had to deal with?

PROACTIVE COMMUNICATION WITH PARENTS IS VITAL

We're also relational with our parents. Each week in the offseason every coach writes a short note 'to the parents of' on our stationary and we mail out. We've gotten good feedback on this. It takes just a few minutes and we make sure all get a note mailed to them at one time or another.

I won't spend time detailing all of these, but communication is king to develop relationships. Our parents hear about Grapevine football year-round. We get our message out a lot, in a lot of different ways.

In late July, we have a Football 101 for Moms event and it's one of the most fun things we do. We bring in different people who the moms want to hear from before the beginning of the season. Our speakers each get 10 minutes to do their presentation and then each gets five minutes for Q&A.

We invite our team doctor, a nutritionist, a football official and our team chaplain. Our offensive and defensive coordinators speak about the basic schemes we run. Our booster club president talks about the role of the booster club. The moms get a 'pregame meal' like their sons eat on game day.

Other ways we communicate with our parents:

- August parent meeting
- Remind 101
- Facebook
- Twitter
- Website

I mentioned Coach Snyder of Kansas State earlier in this book. He gave me a great idea they do to be relational with their parents. Each position coach calls the parents of his players once a month. What a great idea! Twelve times a year the parents are hearing from their son's position coach!!

The coaches have a form they fill out after the conversation and turn it in to Coach Snyder so he also knows what was discussed. He says they have learned a lot about things about the past of their players. Things a player has gone through that the staff wouldn't have known about without speaking with the parents. We will steal this and implement it.

Answer emails and phone calls the same day you receive them. This needs to be a priority. It's professional and respectful. Have I ever forgotten to answer an email? Yes. But it's rare and not the way things should be done.

When I get home I try hard to be AT HOME. You should as well. It's possible to be a great coach and a great family man, but you must be intentional about both. When you get home, disconnect from the outside world as much as possible and put your focus on where it needs to be - your family. Brian Cain calls this "digital detox." 'Be where your feet are' and focus on what's important - your family. I'm a work in progress on this because I love most everything about coaching, but our spouses deserve our attention and our children really do grow up so fast!

SUCCESS VS. SIGNIFICANCE

I will talk about Payday later in the book, but payday is about success. I interviewed Dr. Rob Gilbert from Montclair State about topics for this book and he talked about the difference in success and significance.

"Success is driven by beating others," he said. "Significance is to help others win. A successful coach will have trophies in the school trophy case, but a significant coach will have players who will come back and visit them because he/she made a difference in their life. A 'real' coach strives to be significant." I couldn't agree more. When we are retired from coaching we will want to look back and think about all the lives we impacted. Do we want to add some 'gold balls' to the trophy case? Of course, but winning is a byproduct of relationships anyway so the more you are significant as a coach, the more your teams will win.

FORMING A 'BAND OF BROTHERS' BETWEEN TEAMMATES

> *"Why do soldiers fight? Not for the hatred of those in front of them, but the love for the those behind them."*
>
> **G.K. Chesterton**

Being a B-17 crewmember one of the toughest jobs in World War II and definitely the deadliest. Casualty rates early in the war (from 1942-43) were a staggering 65%. The numbers did improve as we figured out better ways to protect our flying fortresses, but death rates were very high compared to 3.29% for the Marines, 2.25% for the Army and .41% for the Navy.

A tour of duty was 25 missions. All total, it was estimated the average crewman had a 1-in-4 chance of actually completing his tour. Not only was death common, hundreds of thousands were wounded and more than 21,000 were taken prisoner.

The flying conditions for the B-17s were also not for the faint of heart. The planes were unheated and open to outside air. As the planes rose in elevation the temperature dropped. Crewmen wore electrically-heated suits and multiple pairs of gloves, but the temps could reach 60 below!!

When sorties went deep into enemy territory, it could be an eight-hour mission. Anxious eyes would search the sky for enemy fighters armed with machine guns, canons and rockets. Surface-to-air missiles were always a fear.

When a soldier's 25 missions were completed he had the option of being honorably discharged or reenlist. After such a harrowing tour of duty some opted for discharge, but many stayed and continued to take the risk on the B-17 bombers.

The military decided to research why so many stayed and reenlisted and the findings were not what they expected. The researchers expected the primary answers to be; hatred of the enemy, love for country, or to make their parents, wife or girlfriend proud. Actually, the number one reason the flyers stayed was because of their fellow crewmen. They had bonded together and did not want to let each other down. Some said if they left they knew an inexperienced crewman would take their place and jeopardize the safety of their buddies.

This is one reason we won the war. This type of bond is what every coach should preach to his/her team. FAMILY.

UNITY SHARING

When I sat down with Coach Snyder, I asked him specific questions about culture and relationships. "What is the best way you have your team bond together as teammates?" Sometimes when I pose questions to coaches they hesitate and gather their thoughts (like I would), but Coach Snyder did not flinch or think about his answer. Immediately, he responded with, "Unity sharing."

Unity sharing is a post-practice exercise. Each day the coaches pair off the players and have them spend one minute answering a question to each other. They are always paired with a different teammate. "We have around 120 guys so in 120 practices (in season and out of season) they will talk to every member of the team."

Examples of questions are:
· Describe your relationship with your dad?
· What is the most disappointing time in your life?
· Describe your ideal career / job you would like to have in 10 years.

"We make sure our men understand trust has to be valued. Your teammate is only telling you this and it is not for anyone else. To receive this type of information requires you to be trustworthy. It stays between the two of you."

This is why I love visiting with other coaches about the intangibles. There is no doubt trust will be built up and the more we know about each other the more we don't want to let them down. We will add unity sharing to our program and I'm excited to see it deepen the relationships between our players.

FAMILY QUIZ GAME

When I arrived at Plano East I realized very quickly as a whole our team didn't know each other very well. As I mentioned, East has a fractured system with two 9-10 campuses that feed into one large 11-12 campus.

In our summer conditioning we ran sprints to finish most workouts. I began to quiz the guys to see how much they knew about their teammates. They didn't know much about each other.

As they would be at the line I would say, "John, tell me about Eric's siblings. How many brothers and sisters does he have?" If Eric couldn't answer we would back up 5 yards. They got better as the weeks went by. I started noticing before we would begin our sprints they would quickly question each other about their families.

THE BUDDY SYSTEM

This is a great way to get your players to encourage each other during practice. Put the names of everyone on offense in a hat or sack. Have each player pull out a name and not say who it is. Do the same with the defense.

During practice his job is to encourage the player whose name he drew out, but not make it obvious. At the end of practice we ask guys to guess who their 'encourager' was. Everyone's goal should be to have more than one player think he was his guy.

PHYSICAL TOUCH BONDS TEAMMATES

Do good teams touch each other more than bad teams? Yes. In a 2009 study of NBA teams they found good teams butt-slap, fist-bump, high-five, chest bump and hug more than bad teams.

The study was called: "Tactile Communication, Cooperation, and Performance: An Ethological Study of the NBA," and was published by Michael W. Kraus, Cassy Huang, and Dacher Keltner.

The scientist studied and recorded every physical contact made by each team in the NBA for a short stretch of the season. Their findings found that, with a few exceptions, good teams were the most 'touchy-feely.' The bad teams had the least physical contact.

The teams who met in the NBA finals that year — the Lakers and Celtics — were at the top on the 'touchy meter.'

Did the findings hold true for the best players in the league as well? Yes. Perennial All-Star and 2004 League MVP Kevin Garnett was the touchiest player, followed by Chris Bosh and Carlos Boozer. "Within 600 milliseconds of shooting a free throw, Garnett has reached out and touched four guys", Dr. Keltner said.

The very next year a different study was done on the effect of touch in the NBA and the Dallas Mavericks led the league in touching each other. They also won the title that year.

Platonic touching is important. One of the major functions of touch is to promote trust and cooperation. If you want someone to say yes to a question touch him or her on the arm. When a waitress touches her customers, male or female, on the wrist or arm, they tend to get bigger tips.

Leaders touch their people. Don Meyer is the winningest all-time coach in NCAA men's basketball history. He recently retired from Northern State University in Aberdeen, South Dakota. Coach Meyer had a goal of 8-12 'touches' per day both personally and professionally.

Coach Art Briles spoke of the importance of touching at a clinic a few years back. He said his was to touch *every player, every day*. He made sure he high-fived, fist-bumped, butt-slapped, etc. every one of his players.

Before Baylor practices the strength coaches make a 'human tunnel' to high five players and coaches as they enter the field. Even at Orange Theory they encourage adults (who don't know each other) working out to high-five or fist-bump others as they switch stations. We need human contact for motivation. Great teams are intentional about it.

APPRECIATION

Appreciation is to show gratitude to others, especially in a non-verbal manner. We want to make sure we not only have a great bond with each other, but show others we appreciate them as well.

University of Texas men's basketball coach Shaka Smart ties his core values to a specific day of the week like we do. Monday is Appreciation for the Longhorns. Cody Daniel, a writer for SB Nation, interviewed Coach Smart before the 2015 season.

Every Monday, Smart gives his players homework. Each must demonstrate nonverbal appreciation to someone that day. It can be a hug, a pat on the back, or even a smile. Each player must report back the next day.

"Its tough to do," says, Demarcus Holland, who will fulfill his duty by hugging the strength coaches, "but he wants to hear about it."

Thursday is our day to show others appreciation. We assign our guys to show nonverbal appreciation to different groups each week by having them take a 'selfie' with the person they are thanking. We have a closed Facebook group for our team and have them post to it. Groups we have targeted are: members of their family, favorite teacher, custodial/cafeteria staff or a classmate who has helped them in the past.

The first time I asked our guys to take a pic and thank the custodians they were turned down by a few. The custodians weren't sure what was going on. Sad, but they weren't used to students thanking them for their service. This is not only great for our custodians, but for our players to learn the importance of honoring everyone who is part of the 'team.'

SMU HOSPITALITY

During the past two years I've been able to visit quite a few spring football practices held by the SMU Mustangs. Chad Morris is the head coach and has the best open-door policy of any place I have ever visited. To say they treat high school coaches special would be an understatement.

Morris is a former Texas high school coach and he has a system in place that shows appreciation to anyone that visits. You are made to feel special when you visit by every member of his staff.

Each day from 10 a.m. to 1 p.m., each position coach 'clinics' to several visiting coaches. At 2 p.m., Coach Morris allows all coaches to sit in on his team meeting. Each time I have sat in on a team meeting I have picked up a great team-building thought or strategy.

This year Coach Morris told his players to hurry and get showered after practice so they could meet up with their professor for their Annual Professor's Dinner. This peaked my interest. I started asking questions about what the Professor's Dinner was all about. Each player delivered a hand-written note to their favorite professor inviting him/her to attend practice that day and a dinner in their honor that night. It was a fairly formal affair that was not only appreciated by the faculty, but also teaches the players how to invite and host a special guest at a formal dinner.

This spring we 'piggy-backed' off the Professor's Dinner with an ice cream social after school the day of our spring game. We had tables and chairs set up in the end zone. As teachers arrived the player who invited him/her took their order and made them a sundae. After all the teachers were served, each player one by one announced their guest and told the group why he/she was special. They also took a selfie with their teacher, which we posted on our public Facebook and Twitter channels.

Another way Coach Morris and his staff shows appreciation to the professors is by inviting two of them to travel with the team on out-of-town games.

They 'imbed' with the team. They fly on the charter plane, join in on all meals and even attend player meetings. The coaches have gotten great feedback from the professors on the impact the road trips have made. All are amazed at how much organization and sophistication go into game preparation and all that goes into getting ready to play a game.

CAPTAIN CULTURE AND FAT BURGER

Graham Ryan is a senior on our offensive line. He also serves on our Leadership Council (elected by his teammates) and is one of the top all-around students at Grapevine High School.

I call Graham "Captain Culture." He's one of those special kids who 'gets it.' He's not special because he will be all-state athlete or play college football. He is a hard worker and contributor to our team, but it's the leadership he brings to us that makes Graham one of our special guys.

Our field house is at Mustang Stadium and we practice there each day. It's about three quarters of a mile from the school. There's a bus that will take the guys who don't have a car to school after our morning practices, but most drive their own vehicle. We talk to our guys about making sure everyone has a ride if they are late out of the shower and miss the bus.

One of our managers, Darius, did not have a car. In fact, Darius had just moved here from Waco and didn't really have any friends on the team when the season started. One day we were talking in the office and one of our coaches mentioned that every day Graham would take Darius to school so he didn't have to ride the bus. Lots of times they would stop at the 7-11 nearby and Graham would even buy Darius a drink and something to eat.

This past spring, Graham approached me about Darius suiting up for the spring game. All on his own, Graham decided it would be a great thing for Darius to be a part of our game and play one play, making sure he scores a touchdown.

Darius had never played football and was nervous about it. In true Darius humbleness he told me, "Coach, I'm afraid I will mess it up and let you down." I told him if he didn't do it he would be letting me down.

Our spring game is open to the public. We play in in the evening and always have a good turnout. We estimated our crowd at around 1,500 this year. The word got out about Darius playing and some of our cheerleaders even made signs for him. We devised a special play for Darius to score. I asked him what his favorite meal is and he said "Fat Burger". There you go, our new special play for Darius to score would be called "Fat Burger."

It was a reverse where our quarterback faked to our running back then handed the ball to Darius. The entire team was in on it. Once Darius got the ball we had guys diving and pretending to try to tackle him, but just miss. Darius scored from 40 yards out, smiling from ear to ear.

After the game when all were on the field Darius had lots of people congratulating him and even taking pictures with him. He was on Cloud Nine, reliving his touchdown. He was the last player to take off his uniform that night.

Darius has a lifetime memory because of one person who cared enough to make it happen, Graham Ryan. After this season Graham will enroll at Texas A&M and be in the Corp of Cadets. We will miss him not only because he makes us better on the offensive line, but because of his leadership and his commitment to our core value of family. I can't wait to see how Graham attacks the next chapter in his life in the Corp.

I believe Graham would have done all of this without the values we teach everyday. He is that type of person. But, we make guys like Graham a big deal in our program. We celebrate it when a teammate shows love to another teammate.

CHAPTER 7 REVIEW
LESSON #4 FAMILY AND APPRECIATION

☐ True leadership develops unselfish teams that play for each other. This is the most important and toughest job for any coach.

☐ The TEAM, the TEAM, the TEAM

☐ I want coaches who are 'kid magnets' on my staff. Professionals who develop relationships and sincerely enjoy people.

☐ Leaders are proactive with communication to parents.

☐ Success or Significance? For a 'real' coach this is an easy question.

☐ Its not the dislike of the other team that will create a great bond for your team, it is the love for each other.

☐ Physical touch is something every leader should do daily. Have a goal to touch the arm or shoulder of half your team each day.

☐ Find ways for your players to show appreciation to others. Teachers, support staff, family...everyone and celebrate it when they do.

CHAPTER 8

LESSON #5 – DISCIPLINE

> *"Discipline is the bridge from goals to accomplishment."*
>
> **Jim Rohn**

Back on January 9, 2016, the Pittsburgh Steelers were leading 15-0 after three quarters against the rival Cincinnati Bengals in an AFC Wild-Card Playoff game. The game was borderline boring and I almost stopped watching it. I'm sure glad I stayed with it because lots of teachable moments happened in the last quarter I was able to share with my team.

If you like offense (like most of us do) it was tough to find much to keep you interested. Steelers' QB Ben Roethlisberger had been knocked out of the game and the very inexperienced Landry Jones was quarterbacking the team. The Bengals were struggling to make first downs, much less score points.

The Bengals finally got something going in the fourth quarter; they scored a touchdown and field goal on consecutive drives to close the gap to 15-10. Amazingly, with their backup quarterback, A.J. McCarron, in the game, the Bengals scored again late to go up 16-15.

The Steelers had 1:50 to respond and Jones promptly threw an interception. It should have been "ball game."

Culture Defeats Strategy

Cincinnati was about to win their first playoff game in 25 years. All the Bengals had to do was run out the clock.

They couldn't.

Jeremy Hill fumbled the ball giving it back to the Steelers with 1:23 left in the game.

With their hopes fading, Roethlisberger trots out. Big Ben had an injured throwing shoulder and couldn't throw the ball more than 10-15 yards. He dinked and dunked four completions to get the Steelers to midfield with only 22 seconds left in the game.

"He was able to go back in the game, but I don't know how far he was able to throw the ball," Pittsburgh coach Mike Tomlin said of his QB. "That's why the last drive looked the way it looked."

The Bengals' meltdown occurred on the next snap. Vontaze Burfict, an inside linebacker, was called for a personal foul penalty. He went high, to the head of receiver Mike Brown, after an incompletion. One reporter said, "Burfict tried to decapitate Brown." It was the correct call without a doubt. The 15-yard penalty would move the ball to the 32-yard line and the Steelers were now in field goal range, although it would've been a 49-yard attempt.

Cincinnati's lack of discipline would continue to haunt them as Adam 'Pac-Man' Jones began arguing the Burfict call with an official. He was flagged 15 more yards. Now the ball was on the 17-yard line, chip-shot distance for any NFL kicker.

Steelers kicker Chris Boswell kicks it through the middle. Now it was 'ball game'.

The headlines from that game included:
"Bengals Lose All Control"
"Bengals Have Playoff Meltdown For the Ages"
"This is Bengals' Worst Playoff Loss Ever",
"Blame Marvin Lewis for the Bengals Out-of-Control Playoff Meltdown"
"Undisciplined Cincinnati Bengals Still Wayward After Playoff Loss to Steelers."

I can take losing to a better opponent, but giving a game away due to lack of discipline is a tough pill to swallow.

Three major things happened that are all due to a lack of discipline;

1. The Fumble — A disciplined runner would have had two hands on the ball and made sure it wasn't coming out. The clock ticking down was the only objective.
2. The Penalty — Burfict let his ego get in front of what was best for the team. He was more concerned about being the alpha male (which we like most of the time) than being smart.
3. The Subsequent Penalty — As bad as things were the Bengals still had a chance to pull it out. Then Jones loses all self-control and gets a 15-yard penalty for confronting an official about the preceding call.

I am not the 'king of self-control'. Officials and I do not exchange Christmas cards on a regular basis, but a total collapse cannot happen. Pressure makes the pipe burst.

Three Bengals players failed their teammates, coaches and fans during the pressure of the playoffs.

> *"More games are lost than won."*
>
> **Bill Parcells**
> **Former NFL Head Coach**
> **Patriots, Giants, Jets, Cowboys**

DISCIPLINE IS TIMELESS

Discipline has been a favorite word for coaches since sport began. In biblical times, Paul talks about the importance of discipline in 1 Corinthians 9:25-27.

"All athletes are disciplined in their training. They do it to win a prize that will fade away, but we do it for an eternal prize. So I run with purpose in every step. I am not just shadowboxing. I discipline my body like an athlete, training it to do what it should."

Early coaches in all sports had a military influence guiding their philosophies for program building. The 'Mount Rushmore' of 20th century football coaches — Amos Alonzo Stagg, Pop Warner, Knute Rockne and Vince Lombardi — preached the importance of discipline. John Wooden's sixth block on his famous pyramid deals with discipline and self-control. Think about all the great coaches in the past and today. All had discipline. It's the foundation.

Discipline is defined as the practice of training people to obey rules or a code of behavior, using punishment to correct disobedience — 'conscious control over a lifestyle — mental self-control used in directing or changing behavior, learning something, or training for something.'

Discipline cannot be a bad word in your program. Many young people think their manhood is being dishonored if they are disciplined. We talk about being a disciplined team as a badge of honor. We sell our guys on the importance of discipline in their daily lives. I tell our team they will be 'Uber' successful later in life if they will apply the discipline they learn from our program to their career. Anything you emphasize you will get. We emphasize the importance of discipline.

Discipline for us is self-control, finishing what you start, obedience. Discipline is doing the little things right on a daily basis. Attention to detail.

THE MAKING OF THE ARABIAN HORSE

The most expensive horses are only valuable because they have been trained. One of the most famous, and expensive, breed of horse is the Arabian. The purebred Arabian horse is striking in its appearance. With its finely-chiseled head, dished face, long arching neck and high tail carriage. Its entire presence exudes energy, intelligence, courage and nobility. Every time an Arabian moves in its famous "floating trot," he announces to the world his proud, graceful nature.

Legend has it the Arabian horse breed was started from one horse that was disciplined above all others. The story has it that an Arabian king who lived a few thousand years before Christ sent out 100 of his best men and told them they had a year to search 'high and wide' for the best horse they could find.

After a year, all 100 men were back from their search, each with a beautiful horse to present to the king. The king took the horses and trained each of them to respond to his whistle. After a couple of months of this daily training, no matter what they were doing, if they heard the whistle the horses would run to the king.

It was time for the true test of discipline and self-control. The king had a pen built on a hill that overlooked a large pool of water. After all the horses were put in the pen the king withheld food and water. The pond was probably 100 yards away, but the horses could see and smell it.

All of them became hungry and of course, very thirsty in the intense Arabian heat. After a day they began behaving differently. Many of them were noticeably irritated. After two days, the horses were biting and snapping at each other. It was obvious they were in dire straights and would have done anything to get out of the pen and sprint down the hill to the pool of water.

During the third day, the king had one of his men open the gate and release the horses. They bolted out and down the hill. All were sprinting as fast as their weakened bodies would allow. They were desperate to quench their.

The king was standing at the bottom of the hill opposite of the pool of water. He watched the horses sprint for a few seconds allowing them to get three quarters of the way to the pond. He then blew his whistle. One horse

responded. One horse resisted his need for water and stopped his path to it. One horse turned and sprinted to the king. From this horse the world's finest breed was developed — the Arabian horse.

NEED 3%'ers WHO ARE HEROES

One of my favorite graphics is a pyramid I received in the mail from Chad Morris at SMU a year or so ago. Many colleges send mail-outs to high school head coaches advertising their school with a motivational quote or short story. This graphic lists the work characteristics of the top 3% of Americans who are 'Uber' achievers. It also describes the 10% who want to be special, the 60% who are mediocre, and the 27% who won't make it.

The pyramid illustrates the different types of recruits even a prestigious program like Ohio State gets year to year. I have heard Urban Meyer speak on this pyramid and talk about the recruits they sign each year. One would think because they recruit nationally and are normally at the top of the recruiting rankings they would only get the most disciplined and driven to succeed players, but Coach Meyer says this pyramid holds true most of the time.

We talk to our team about these characteristics. We make sure they understand to be 'normal' isn't what we must have to make our program great again like it was in the 90's (under Coach Mike Sneed).

To get back to winning state championships, we have to have players that want to be special. Self-discipline and allowing us to make them into our version of an Arabian horse gives us a chance to be special.

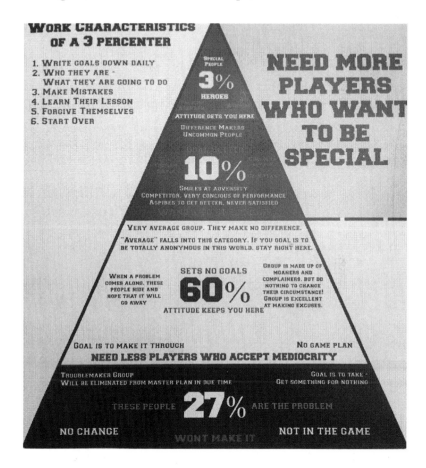

THE COST OF BEING UNDISCIPLINED

The Bengals' playoff debacle was easy to breakdown on the cost of the lack of discipline, but there are so many examples of athletes and coaches who have derailed their career because he they could not discipline themselves also.

> *"Undisciplined people are slaves to their own weaknesses."*
>
> **Unknown**

One that comes to mind fairly quickly is the great Woody Hayes in the 1978 Gator Bowl. The Buckeyes were down 17-15 late in the game, but were in field goal range. Ohio State freshman quarterback, Art Schlichter, threw an interception to Clemson linebacker Charlie Bauman. Schlichter tackled Bauman on the Ohio State sideline. Hayes lost his 'stuff.' He grabbed Bauman and said to him, "You SOB, I just lost my job!"

Coach Hayes was a brilliant coach. His career record is 205-61-15. His teams were disciplined, but his lack of self-discipline did cost him his job. More importantly, it cost him his legacy. He is still remembered by many, but the punch comes to mind very quickly when you think back to Coach Hayes.

It takes very little research to find more recent examples. Tiger Woods would have been known as the greatest golfer of all time if infidelity hadn't totally derailed his career. He lost his good name, his swing, and millions in endorsements. He hasn't been the same golfer since.

Johnny Manziel is throwing his career away because of his immaturity and lack of self-control. He was absolutely the most electric college football player I've ever watched. I used to think of him as the 'Michael Jordan' of the SEC, but he doesn't have the self-discipline to focus on football more than partying in nightclubs.

If you watched the 2016 NFL Draft, it was sad to see the

saga of Laremy Tunsil. His lack of self-discipline embarrassed his entire family, the Ole Miss program and the estimated cost of falling from the #1 overall pick to the #13 pick is estimated to be close to $14 million.

In 1991, I attended the Nike Coach of the Year Clinic in Dallas. I got to hear the great Johnny Majors, former head football coach of the Tennessee Volunteers, speak on the kicking game.

My one memory of Coach Majors' talk was the type of player coaches should use when they personnel their special teams units.

"There is lots of yardage exchanged in every play in the kicking game. Make sure you have disciplined players who will execute their role. If you have a fast player, but he will not stay in his lane when covering kickoffs, do not put him on the kickoff unit. He will get you beat."

Coach Majors added another nugget about the importance of discipline in the kicking game.

"All penalties in the kicking game are big. Most are 15-yard penalties. Do not use undisciplined players in your special teams. Undisciplined players get penalties and penalties in the kicking game will get you beat, quick."
Undisciplined teams are easy to spot. They commit too many penalties. Pre-snap and personal foul penalties are cardinal sins in Grapevine. One of our coaches will make a penalty cut-up each week and we watch it as a team on Thursdays. We also keep a running spreadsheet of penalties and post in the locker room for all to see.

The Air Force Academy football team led the country a few years ago with only three penalties for twenty-four yards a game. It makes sense that the discipline of a military academy football team would lead the nation in fewest penalties and yards. Although it is tough to achieve, this is our weekly goal for penalties.

A clean locker room is also an indicator of discipline. Jennings Teel was my superintendent when I was the coach in Mason and was a former football coach. One of his stops was in Sweetwater where he coached under legendary W.T. Stapler.

He told me every time they played on the road, coach Stapler would find a way to get into the home team's locker room. If the locker room was clean and organized he knew they would be facing a disciplined team. All my teams have heard this story, usually when we are bear-crawling for the locker room not being up to our standard.

> *"Discipline yourself and others won't need to."*
>
> **John Wooden**
> **Former Men's Basketball Coach**
> **UCLA Bruins**

SELF-CONTROL

When we go through our core values, self-discipline is where we take our pinky finger, point it at our sternum and say, "Count on me." Count on me is saying 'I have the character to withstand the desires or impulses of what I want now to achieve long-term success.

Delaying gratification is essential to long-term success. This point has been proved with science.

In 1972, Stanford researcher Walter Mischel became famous when he devised his 'cookie experiment.' Mischel took 4-year-olds and gave them two options: they could eat their choice of three treats now (cookie, marshmallow or pretzel) or wait 15 minutes and get two of the same treat.

Mischel told them, "I want to give you a treat, but I have to leave for a while. You can have one now, or if you can wait when I return you can have two."

Mischel left the treat in front of the child as he exited the office. He returned 15 minutes later. If they had not eaten the treat he gave them the two he promised. Many could not resist the temptation.

Mischel tracked the kids as they went through school and entered adulthood. The children who had the self-control to wait for him to reenter the room had much more success than those who eat the one treat immediately.

"It was twice as powerful a predictor of what their IQ scores were at age four or their SAT scores were later."

Brian Johnson's Optimizer (great stuff, I encourage all to look into) talks about this principal in his Philosopher's Notes on Daniel Goleman's book "Emotional Intelligence."

Goleman identifies the ability to delay gratification as one of the keys to emotional intelligence. He adds, "There is perhaps no psychological skill more fundamental than resisting impulse."

A great player who is great 'most of the time' frustrates me more than anything. The lack of self-control is almost always the reason for their mistake.

> *"Many of life's failures are people who did not realize how close they were to success when they gave up."*
>
> **Thomas Edison**
> **Inventor**

ATTENTION TO DETAIL

The first year to do a boot camp was in the offseason of 2011. We had an ROTC program at Poteet so I went to them and asked if they would help us 'whip them into shape,' so to speak. This was a great decision. The ROTC instructors 'got after them' during the first 10 minutes of boot camp as they got dressed and in formation for inspection.

The 'drill sergeants' did a great job of finding the little things to correct. If shoes were not tied ... pushups, not looking them in the eyes ... pushups, not moving fast enough when getting down to do pushups ... more pushups!

Each time they went down for a pushup the players had to shout 'attention to detail.' On the way up they would shout 'teamwork is the key.' We don't have access to these men anymore, but we still use this today when our guys are doing pushups in boot camp.

I played tight end at Louisiana-Monroe from 1985-88. The tight ends worked with the offensive line most of the time. J.B. Grimes was the offensive line coach and to this day all of us who were lucky enough to play for Coach Grimes have his phrase "little things" permanently engrained in our heads.

After playing high school football in Tenaha (33 in my graduating class) it was an eye-opener to be around Coach Grimes. He was the most intense, 5-foot-7 offensive line coach in the history of football.

It was always '4th and 1' when Coach Grimes was coaching. His intensity and attention to detail are what made him one of the most respected offensive line coaches in the country.

"It's the little things, men. The little things mean a lot. Your first step must be six inches, not five, not seven ... six inches!!!"

I was very fortunate to be around Coach Grimes for four years. His demand of attention to detail has influenced my coaching from to this day.

> *"Excellence in small things is excellence in all things."*
> **Unknown**

DISCIPLINE TO CORRECT BEHAVIOR

Jim Harbaugh tells of his eye-opening experience with Coach Schembechler after being late to his first team meeting in 1982.

"It was the very first meeting of the freshmen," Harbaugh

recalled. "I was out somewhere and lost track of the time. I got there late. Oh, man. I popped my head in five or 10 minutes late and Bo just exploded. 'WHERE HAVE YOU BEEN?' I just froze. I couldn't get a word out. 'WHERE HAVE YOU BEEN?' I mumbled something. I was petrified. He was screaming at me in front of all these guys I had never even met before. He goes, 'You of all people! I can't believe you! Your dad's a coach! I'm gonna call him tonight!' He was enraged. He stormed around. Then he said, 'YOU'LL NEVER PLAY A DOWN OF FOOTBALL HERE! NEVER!"

Times have changed. Coaches are mentors more than drill sergeants.

"There can't be rules without relationships." A good friend of mine, Bob Wager, said this. Bob is the head football coach at Arlington Martin High School in Arlington, Texas. He's exactly right. Years ago respect was a given. Your title granted you the right, in the minds of the athletes, to discipline them. As I mentioned earlier in the book, we are looking for kid magnets. Kid magnets are relational and discipline is much easier when a relationship has been formed.

> *"I don't think discipline is forcing somebody to do something. It's showing them how this is going to help them in the long run. You set rules and you enforce rules. You just tell the athlete that you expect him to do what's right, do the best he can and treat others like he'd like to be treated."*
>
> **Lou Holtz**
> **Former Head Football Coach**
> **Notre Dame**

I tell the team we discipline them because we care about them and love them. I'm going to treat them like my own kids. They've heard this before.

"I love my son, Russ, more than anything. Too much to allow him to not overachieve if he has a moment of lack of self-control or makes a bad choice."

When you relate discipline to correcting behavior because you love them too much to let them fail, they at least have a chance to understand it.

HAVE A SYSTEM IN PLACE TO HANDLE THE DAY-TO-DAY ISSUES THAT NEED TO BE ADDRESSED. LEADERS DON'T MAKE THREATS THEY MAKE PROMISES AND FOLLOW THROUGH.

We meet as a team at the beginning of each season and discuss what the consequences will be for minor infractions. This way when we do have a tardy it is 'cut and dry' what will happen and they feel like they had input of the upcoming consequence.

You must have a system in place to deal with these infractions. Our head wrestling coach, Matt Criner, is also a football coach. He coaches our punters and kickers (a group that is often neglected). In many programs they are off on another field by themselves without anyone to coach them. During games they do not have 'their guy' to help prepare them or give them counsel after a mistake.

One of the biggest advantages to having a smaller role in Coach Criner's football assignment is that it frees him up to be our discipline coach. When we need to change a behavior we have him give our guys some 'tough love' before they join the team. It'll be 5-10 minutes of agility, bear crawls, plate pushes, etc.

Coach Snyder at Kansas State calls this punishment a "P.I." — the price of irresponsibility.

Athletes crave discipline. They may fuss and complain about it at times, but they want boundaries. We all want to know what's acceptable and what expectations we're to meet. We don't have a lot of rules, but we do have standards. We make sure our players and parents know what they are.

You shouldn't discipline your athletes without communicating with them and their parents if it is something more the 'garden variety' infraction. It's easy to do, but it is not the right thing. If you don't communicate with the parents they will hear only one side of the story and it will not be the version you will want them to hear. Most of the time when we meet with the parents and their child it goes very well and things improve.

*Always meet with the parents and the child TOGETHER.

> "Discipline is the highest form of love. If you really love someone, you have to give them the level of discipline they need. Great players crave discipline."
>
> **Tom Izzo**
> **Head Basketball Coach**
> **Michigan State University**

I am lucky we don't have many discipline issues at Grapevine. Deciding how long to allow a player to disrupt the team with his bad choices is definitely one of the biggest struggles head coaches face. It's very easy for assistant coaches to say, "that guy is killing us, if it were me I would get rid of him." I was guilty of this as an assistant coach, but when it's your decision alone, it's tough. Our program is good for young people. The ones who do turn it around are success stories we all feel good about.

Those success stories are not as common as I wish they were. I've made the mistake of not being patient enough with players who lack self-discipline. As I get older, I want to see the 'teachable moments' in their bad choices, but I have to admit ... things usually don't work out for the best.

Usually, the guys with little self-control take up most of your time and they get you beat in the fourth quarter anyway. Do you give them one more chance or do you cut them loose so they don't hurt your team chemistry?

This I am sure of ... if you're going to stand in front of your team and preach the importance of discipline, you must have the stomach to make the tough call. Coaches who do not follow through with what they say they'll do lose credibility. Once you lose credibility with your team, all is lost as a leader. We're going to line up with guys who 'can't live without it' and not cater to the 2% Coach Saban talked about. I know it can be a tough decision to let someone go, but if you stand firm with your 'all in' guys, they will stand firm with you.

I was talking with two members of our leadership council recently and they both said, "This is why we love being a part of this team. All of us are treated the same and no one is put above the team." It made my day to hear this.

> *"Discipline is not punishment. Discipline is changing someone's behavior."*
>
> **Nick Saban**
> **Head Football Coach**
> **Alabama Crimson Tide**

The Michigan State Spartans play disciplined football. They don't beat themselves with stupid penalties or unforced errors. Their head coach, Mark Dantonio, keeps a 'discipline clock' on the wall in their practice facility. He resets it each time a player breaks a team rule or otherwise gets in trouble.

We will get us a 'discipline clock' for this upcoming season and put it up next to our weekly countdown clock in our varsity locker room. Our leadership council and I will create the criteria or standard for what will make the clock stop; tardies, unexcused absences, etc. We will strive to keep the clock running this season. I love it.

DISCIPLINE SETS LEADERS AND TEAMS APART

In 2015 we were playing on the road in Fort Worth. As we were warming up it was raining hard and the forecast gave no indication of letting up. The opposing coach and I agreed to start the game early. I ran over and gathered up the team and told them we were about to get the game going. We were favored to win fairly easy, but I did not want to see us 'slop around' and play undisciplined.

I used this story when I spoke to them; "When a ship leaves port it has set it's course. It doesn't matter if the weather is bad. It doesn't need to have line of sight or have good weather to stay on its course. When the ship captain finally sees his port of call his journey is more than 99% complete. He didn't need to see his destination. The captain used his instruments and calculations to guide him throughout. We can't worry about the weather or anything else that happens tonight. We set our course back in offseason, fall camp and this week of practice. Keep your discipline and do not focus on anything but your job."

> **"Habits reflect the mission."**
>
> **Sign leading to the field at**
> **Lincoln Financial Field in Philadelphia**

Bill Parcells has a list of three things that sets disciplined people apart:

· The capacity to get past distractions
· The willingness to condition mind and body for
  the task at hand
· The ability to keep your poise when those around you
  are losing theirs

Playing in bad weather is an advantage for a disciplined team. Anything out of the ordinary like rain, a lightning delay, homecoming festivities, Saturday game, etc. hinders undisciplined teams.

There are lots of benefits our guys will get out of being in our program, but self-discipline and attention to detail will be somewhere near the top of the list. Getting ahead in our society is not hard today. Hard work, doing the little things and attention to detail are three things it takes and they learn all three with us. Business owners tell me over and over how hard it is for them to find employees they can depend on or who are self-starters. Success is about the little things.

> *"Self-disciplined begins with mastery of your thoughts. If you don't control what you think, you can't control what you do. Simply, self-discipline enables you to think first and act afterward."*
>
> **Napoleon Hill**

GUARDING THE TOMB OF THE UNKNOWN SOLDIERS

The 'Tomb of the Unknowns,' located at Arlington National Cemetery in Washington D.C. was dedicated in 1921 and everyday since then, rain or shine (or hurricane), has been guarded by men with the highest of discipline.

Soldiers must be in the 3rd Regiment (the Old Guard) of the U.S. Army to be eligible to volunteer for this duty. That's the easy part. The rest of it requires supreme discipline and attention to detail.

Physically, soldiers should be between 5'10" and 6'3" in height. They're flexible with these requirements; a highly qualified candidate who is 5'9" will not be turned away. There is no waist requirement, but there is an unspoken rule of "if it does not fit on the rack, you are too fat."

Training is rigorous. All 'newmen' are given basic instructions on uniform prep, the walk sequence and behavioral expectations. The average training to become a guard takes around eight months.

Newmen train 12 hours a day. They also have homework learning everything they can about the history of the Tomb of the Unknowns. They do not watch television, talk to the public, talk to other guards (unless spoken to or they are asking a question) or even acknowledge jokes. Their training is generally at night when the cemetery is closed to the public.

During training the 'newmen' are tested on three things:

1. Uniform — Trainees may have up to two minor infractions but no major infractions. A minor infraction is if any one item is more than 1/64" out of place. There are more than 100 points per inspection. If this was the criteria for taking a test in school a 97 would be a failing grade! There has never been a 100 given on this inspection.

2. Knowledge — Newmen must memorize a 17-page packet of information on the cemetery and be able to correctly write it out, including punctuation. A passing grade allows for up to 10 mistakes. If even a comma is missed on a page, it's a double fail. Some of the poems they memorize are about the honor of the Tomb of the Unknown Soldiers.

3. Performance — There are more than 200 points of inspection for the actual guarding of the tomb. They may have two minor infractions, but no

major. The goal is 72 beats per minute, from foot placement on the mat to cadence.

When they pass they become fully qualified and earn a Tomb Guard Identification Badge. They are now known as a Sentinel, the second-rarest rank in the military. Less than 630 badges have ever been issued.

Things do not get easier when they become a full-fledged guard. At every single guard change the upcoming sentinel is inspected and evaluated. At any point, no matter how experienced a guard is, if his weapon touches the plaza outside of weapons inspection he is released from being a tomb guard.

A sentinel will normally own three uniforms; one to wear, one to prepare to wear for duty and one for rain. There is no rank on a sentinel's uniform because we do not know the rank of the unknowns and the sentinels cannot outrank them. On average, it takes a newman 12 hours to prepare a uniform for the plaza, but only five or six hours for a sentinel.

The schedule for the guards is time-consuming. They are on 24-hour duty every other day, but during the 'off' days they continue to study, prepare and shine anything that can be shined. The only true off day they get is once every eight days.

> "*Freedom is a light for which many men have died in darkness.*"
>
> **Tomb of the Unknown Soldier
> of the Revolutionary War**

When the sentinels perform their duty of guarding the tombs, it is discipline personified. They take 21 steps because it alludes to the 21-gun salute, the highest honor given any military or foreign dignitary.

After the 21 steps are taken the sentinel does not execute an about face, they first stop for 21 seconds, click their heels, then turn and face the Tomb for 21 seconds. They then click their heels, turn and face the mat while also changing their weapon to the outside shoulder. They mentally count 21 seconds again, click their heels and step off another 21 steps down the mat. The sentinel faces the tomb at each end of the 21-step walk for 21 seconds. This is repeated over and over until the Guard Change ceremony begins. This change occurs every 30 minutes in the summer and every hour in the winter.

This duty lasts one to one and a half years. After their tour is over and they leave the tomb, they still are expected to maintain the honor of being a tomb guard. Many leave and become members of the Army Rangers Special Forces.

All exiting guards are given a wreath pin that is worn on their lapel signifying they served as guard of the tomb. There are only 400 presently worn. The guard must obey these rules for the rest of his/her life or give up the wreath pin. Felonies, DUI, etc. have caused some guards to lose their badge. If they do commit an offense their name is stricken from the record of being a guard for the tomb.

CHAPTER 8 REVIEW
LESSON #5 DISCIPLINE

- Discipline is timeless. Make sure your team values discipline.

- There are so many examples of players and teams who do not have self-discipline. The worst loss is not having less talent than your opponent, it's having less discipline and self-control.

- The Air Force Academy is the 'gold standard' for disciplined football. Three penalties a game for 24 yards. They do not beat themselves.

- Discipline will only occur if attention to detail and the little things are stressed daily.

- Discipline is about correcting behavior and not punishing. Discipline is love.

- Anything out of the 'norm' will expose undisciplined teams.

CHAPTER 9

LESSON #6 – FINISH

> *"The Cowards Never Started / The Weak Died on the Way / Only the Strong Arrived / They Were the Pioneers."*
>
> **Quote from a Nebraska memorial to those who traveled in the wagon trains along the Oregon and California trails to settle the West.**

A MESSAGE TO GARCIA

When war broke out between Spain and the United States, it was very necessary to communicate quickly with the leader of the Insurgents. Garcia was somewhere in the mountain fastnesses of Cuba - no one knew where. No mail or telegraph could reach him. The President must secure his co-operation, and quickly.

What to do! Someone said to the President, "There's a fellow by the name of Rowan who will find Garcia for you, if anybody can." Rowan was sent for and given a letter to be delivered to Garcia.

How "the fellow by name of Rowan" took the letter, sealed it up in an oil-skin pouch, strapped it over his heart, in four days landed by night off the coast of Cuba from an open boat, disappeared into the jungle, and in three weeks came out on the other side of the island, having traversed a hostile country on foot, and having delivered his letter to Garcia, are things I have no special desire now to tell in detail.

The point I wish to make is this: McKinley gave Rowan a letter to be delivered to Garcia; Rowan took the letter and did not ask, "Where is he?" By the Eternal!

There is a man whose form should be cast in deathless bronze and the statue placed in every college in the land. It is not book-learning young men need, nor instruction about this or that, but a stiffening of the vertebrae which will cause them to be loyal to a trust, to act promptly, concentrate their energies; do the thing — "Carry a message to Garcia!"

Elbert Hubbard wrote the essay 'A Message to Garcia'. The passage above is only a portion of it, but it's a powerful message indeed. We've talked about the essay with our team. Talent is common, but finding people to finish is uncommon.

Employers are just as desperate as coaches to find those who will follow instructions, take the initiative to overcome obstacles, work without supervision and follow through to finish the job. I say it every July in our first coaches meeting of the year ... assistant coaches who will finish assignments without being prompted are priceless and rare. If you are an aspiring coach who wants to lead one day, the best take home from this book is to FIND GARCIA on every assignment.

FINISH DEFINED

Finish is to bring to an end or completion of a task. Finishing is non-negotiable. It's easy to not finish things. In fact, most people don't.

Having a great idea is not enough. Brian Cain encouraged me to write this book at a Peak Performance conference he hosted in Las Vegas.

"Nobody is going to give you permission to write a book, Randy. You have to decide if you are willing to put in the hundreds of hours and finish a big project."

> *"It's the start that stops most people."*
>
> **Brian Cain**
> **Peak Performance Coach**

Writing this book has helped me in several ways. I have learned more about culture and leadership by focusing on it for the past several weeks. I've also learned I have the discipline to stop watching television at night and finish a major project. When I was researching the concept of finish, one article I came upon was how many gamers are not finishing their games.

7% of AMERICAN ADULTS USED A SOCIAL NETWORKING SITE ON A REGULAR BASIS IN 2005. THAT NUMBER HAD INCREASED TO 65% IN 2015.

What is the world coming to? Seriously, it is where we are now culturally. We don't finish much anymore because we can all hit the reset button. We have so many distractions and things that are taking our time that we don't have time to finish.

Facebook and Twitter is a distraction for most people throughout the day. We check our smartphones on average 212 times a day! Next time you stand in line at the grocery store, check to see how many on are on their phones. Raise your hand if you are ever behind someone at a stoplight who doesn't notice it turn green because they're on their phone.

In 2000, the average attention span was 12 seconds. Today it's down to eight seconds. Goldfish have an attention span of nine seconds. We get distracted easily and don't finish.

Leaders must be finishers and leaders must make sure their teams are finishers.

FINISH THE DRILL

For coaches, finish cannot just be your team closing out a game. Finishing is a mindset for everything. I have shouted the phrase, "finish the drill" countless times.

One requirement I have for drills is there has to be an end to it. This may sound elementary, but I have watched other schools practice and at times will see a tackling or blocking drill and the players seem to stop when they feel like they have went far enough. This drives me crazy.

Coaches should wear a whistle and use it to stop the drill when they deem it is finished. In games, we better be finishing through the whistle. I have heard the phrase finish through the 'echo of the whistle.' That's even better.

If we want our players to be trained to go until they hear a whistle then that is how we should train them. Sometimes a whistle is not appropriate to end a drill and a cone is (especially in agility-type drills). This is where I will lose my mind if we don't finish through the cone. Coaches must stand where they can see the finish line. I get fired up just typing this. We yell 'burst' as they sprint through the cone. The burst part of the drill is every bit as important to me as the drill itself. We must ensure they finish the drill!

Hold them accountable when one of your athletes doesn't finish a drill or perform it correctly. Never, ever say 'touch the line' on a drill and not make sure they touch the line. I've seen this happen and for the life of me I can't understand it. When your team knows they will be held accountable to finish ... they will finish.

Another way we finish — we finish the workout. Another head football coach who was very gracious and spoke to me at length was Jerry Kill. Coach Kill was the head football coach at Minnesota until he had to retire due to health problems during the 2015 season.

"I've always taken on rebuilding jobs, I started at a high school in Missouri then to Division II and even at Minnesota. All needed someone to come in and make them tougher and be finishers. One thing we did in the offseason was have our guys draft teams (like we do in boot camp). They would draft and get down to the last few guys. They would say, 'coach, we don't want this guy. We know he is unreliable and we won't be able to count on him.'" Coach Kill would tell them, "Join the club. We have had to deal with them all these months and we can't count on them either. You figure out what to do with them."

The reason they were worried about guys being unreliable is Coach Kill was going to make sure every bit of the workout was finished every day. If there were 85 guys on the offseason roster and they were scheduled to run a 400-meter run at the end of the workout then 85 quarter-miles were going to be ran. If someone was absent or injured a member of his team had to run it for him. Yes sir.

We implemented this during our boot camp this winter. We did give the guys with major injuries a pass, but the guys who did not have surgery were rehabbing a little harder. They had teammates who had to finish the workout for them.

FINISH THE PLAY

Every so often we all learn something so good it changes how we do things for years. I have a growth mindset, I love visiting colleges and high schools and learning how they do things. In the spring of 2015 I was present for Tom Herman's first two spring practices of his head coaching career at the University of Houston. It was in our spring break so I drove down to UH and watched them finish.

Coach Herman and his staff are intense and demand total effort. They coach very hard and their team practiced the same way. The thing that struck me the most was how they finished.

I sat in on offensive line coach Derek Wareheim's meeting with his unit both days. Coach Wareheim does a great job. He really understands how to engage his players and make sure they are locked in during his meeting with them.

On the second day he posted the 'finish grades' for each lineman. They were numerical percentage grades, and I could make out that they were tied to effort, but I hadn't ever heard anyone talking about a finish grade before. Coach Wareheim and I have known each other for years and we have a great relationship so I didn't hesitate to ask him after the meeting what the finish grades were all about.

"Each day we grade their finish anytime we are going in a group or team situation. When the whistle blows, three things can occur; two hands blocking a defender, chasing a defender to block, or a loaf. That's it, nothing else will be factored in on the grade."

They not only grade the offensive line, but the entire team. If a receiver does not get the ball in 'pass skeleton' (7v7) he better turn and find someone to block or he will be marked as loafing. In the days of tempo this is unusual. Before this, we were like most teams and took pride in how many plays we could run during pass skeleton. We have slowed down our pace just a little to demand our guys block as well.

On the defensive side of the ball we also grade finish. Again, three things determine their grade; involved in the tackle, chasing the ball carrier or loaf. We grade practice everyday, but we only grade finish. If a unit has too many loafs they are going to get some tough love to fix it. When we grade game film we grade technique like most people do, but we also grade finish.

I'm always in a hurry. Our practices are intense and every second is accounted for. Grading and emphasizing 'finish' has been a great addition. After years of 'how many plays can we run,' I have to take my whistle off so I don't blow it too quickly because we must take a little extra time to finish. John Wooden always said, "be quick, don't hurry." This means go as fast as you can without being out of control. We were not out of control in the past, but it's been good to slow down a little to insure finish.

TO FINISH FOCUS ON YOUR TEAM

To not finish out a game is tough to think back on. The toughest loss of my career occurred in 2006. It was a second round playoff game between our 10-1 Lone Oak Buffaloes and a very good 10-1 Cisco Lobo squad.

It was my third season in Lone Oak and the 'train was on the track.' We were a talented 2A football team (285 enrollment in high school) and had a great coaching staff. It was our year to make a deep run in the playoffs.

The problem was the same was true of Cisco. They're a traditional power, a force to be reckoned with for any team on their side of the bracket.

I have tried to block this game from my memory. Even thinking back 10 years later is no fun. I do remember this; the game was a war. Both teams traded punches and the score went back and forth. This is before we started playing with tempo, but we were no-huddle and threw the ball some (if only we would have known about tempo back then!).

They were honestly the better team. If we would've played them 10 times we wouldn't have won five, but on this night we had them beat.

> *"Its not the best team that wins, it's the team that plays the best."*
>
> **Brian Cain**
> **Peak Performance Coach**

Late in the game we were down, 31-29, but we're making first downs and driving. With a 1:30 left in the game we had the ball on the 1-inch line!! It was fourth down, with the ball almost touching the goal line.

I called timeout, not to decide what to do, but get everyone focused on the play and make certain everything was in order. We had a fine kicker that I trusted, Cole Middleton, but it wasn't in my head to kick it, or in my nature. To me, there were too many moving parts involved in kicking in what would be even less distance than an extra point.

We were under center occasionally back then and ran the 'tunnel sweep,' a toss to our tailback, but it hits close to the center and is even more effective when it cuts back opposite of the direction the ball is tossed.

The number one reason I wasn't going to kick it was Alex Bowman. Alex was a 6-foot-2, 210-pound sledgehammer with the ball in his hands. He was an All-State performer with a school-record 43 touchdowns his senior year. I was about to give him his chance for No. 44.

During the timeout I was asked by a couple of coaches about kicking the field goal. I was adamant on my decision to run 22 Smash to Bowman. I was confident and wanted to make sure the team knew it wasn't a decision I was unsure about.

An official came over and said, "let's go coach, time to get them back on the field." What happened next is where I made one of the worst mistakes of my career. I out-thought myself in a critical situation.

Back then our tunnel sweep was always on 'two' in our cadence to snap the ball. We had practiced it this way since early August. It was ingrained in them. Just as I was about to break the huddle a thought hit me; let's go on 'first sound' in our cadence. Maybe the defense won't be quite as ready on a quick snap.

Teams finish because of what they've practiced until they have mastered it with hours and hours of repetition. Don Shula calls it 'over-learning.' Instead of catching Cisco, going on 'first sound' caught US off guard. Our timing was disrupted. Bowman took his steps for his path on 22 Smash, but the ball wasn't tossed to him. Blaine Moore, our quarterback, didn't have a good handle on the ball and couldn't toss it to Bowman. Moore tried to make something out of the situation and rolled out to his right, but was tackled for a loss. The timing we had worked on for more than 15 weeks was not in play because I outsmarted myself and tried to catch our opponent off-guard. It was nobody's fault but mine.

Game over. Our crowds were always allowed onto the field after games. It wasn't a fun time for me after the game. One dad thought I called a bootleg. I could hear him yelling, "Why would Jackson call a bootleg? Why wouldn't he give the ball to Bowman if he wasn't going to kick it?" Most thought we should have kicked it. It was a tough situation, but to this day I do not regret calling that play. The mistake was changing the cadence.

In crunch time, when your team must finish, focus on you. Focus on what you do best and don't change anything trying to 'trick' your opponent. It's about your team.

> *"The one thing our program is based upon is finishing. Finish games. Finish your reps. Finish your running. Finish practice strong. Finish the fourth quarter."*
>
> **Will Vlachos**
> **Alabama Crimson Tide Offensive Lineman**

FINISHING IS NOT GIVING IN

Coach Parcells did not see the boxing match between Eugene "Cyclone" Hart and Vito Antuofermo in person, but was told about it years later by a friend and boxing trainer, Teddy Atlas.

The story below is about a favored fighter who didn't 'finish' in a bout in 1977. It was relayed to Michael Lewis by Coach Parcells and appeared in the New York Times in 2006.

"It stuck in his mind and now strikes him as relevant. Seated, at first, he begins to read aloud from the pages: how in this fight 29 years ago Hart was a well-known big puncher, heavily favored against the unknown Vito Antuofermo, how Hart knocked Antuofermo all over the ring, how Antuofermo had no apparent physical gifts except, 'he bled well.'"

"But," Parcells reads, "He had other attributes you couldn't see." Antuofermo absorbed the punishment dealt out by his natural superior, and did it so well that Hart became discouraged. In the fifth round, Hart began to tire, not physically but, mentally. Seizing the moment, Antuofermo attacked and delivered a series of quick blows that knocked Hart down, ending the fight.

"When the fighters went back to their makeshift locker rooms, only a thin curtain was between them. Hart's room was quiet, but on the other side he could hear Antuofermo's corner men talking about who take the fighter to the hospital. Finally he heard Antuofermo say, 'Every time he hit me with that left hook to the body, I was sure I was going to quit. After the second round, I thought if he hit me there again, I'd quit. I thought the same thing after the fourth round. Then he didn't hit me no more.'

"At the moment, Hart began to weep. It was really soft at first, then harder. He was crying because for the first time he understood that Antuofermo had felt just as fatigued as he had and worse. The only thing that separated the guy talking from the guy crying was what they had done. The coward and the hero feel the same emotions. They're both human."

> **"We can do anything we want as long as we stick to it long enough."**
>
> **Helen Keller**

To be a finisher you have to take action. It's the start that stops most people.

If you coach young people you know most of them want results quickly. Hart was the better fighter when he lost to Antuofermo. He didn't stay the course. If he had kept throwing his left hook he would've won the fight.

Results take time. If you have a credit card or a mortgage you understand the law of compound interest. Albert Einstein called it, "the greatest mathematical discovery of all time." Compounding is the exponential growth of an investment.

HEALTH CLUBS SELL MEMBERSHIPS WITH THE INTENT THAT A MERE 18% WILL ACTUALLY USE THEM. ONLY 20% OF NEW JANUARY MEMBERSHIPS ARE STILL BEING USED BY FEBRUARY.

If you were given the choice of three million dollars today or get .1 cent today that doubles for 31 days what would you choose? If you took the penny that doubled after 5 days you would have a whopping .16 cents. After 10 days, the penny doubles to $5.12, almost enough for a combo meal at McDonald's. The three million still looks like the better option.

After 20 days it gets a little better with a sum of $5,242.88. On Day 25, your payout would be $167,772.16. Now the magic of the compound effect takes over. On Day 30, the number goes to $5,368,709.12 and the last day your total goes to a staggering $10,737,418.20!!

Be persistent and finish. If you are a leader, get 1% better each day and stay the course. It will be worth it. There will be people who will be distractions if you are not committed.

When a crab tries to get out of a bucket the other crabs with grab him and pull him back. They will even break his leg if he can to keep him from getting out of the bucket. Like when Brian Cain told me, 'no one is going to give you permission to write a book,' no one is going to give you permission to stay the course and finish.

THE MARATHON MONKS

In Japan, Mount Hiei is a mountain littered with unmarked graves.

The Tendai monks believe that enlightenment can be achieved during your current life, but only through extreme self-denial. To them, enlightenment is a physical challenge that boggles the mind known as the 'Kaihogyo.'

They basically run 1,000 marathons in 1,000 days. The caveat is this; when they reach a certain point of the Kaihogyo and don't finish it, *they must kill themselves*. The monks who have failed to complete the quest are buried on Mount Hiei.

It's a quest that ranks as one of the most difficult

physical challenges in the world. If they achieve the feat they are not only revered, but treated as living saints or human Buddha's, so to speak. Today, those who complete the challenge become celebrities in Japan. Television airs the final stages of their journey live to the nation.

Because of this amount of running involved, the Tendai are often called the "Marathon Monks." But the Kaihogyo is much more than a marathon. The challenge takes place over seven years.

If a monk chooses to undertake this challenge, this is what awaits him ...

Year 1 — The monk must run 18.64 miles (30 km) for 100 straight days.

Year 2 — The monk must again run 18.64 miles (30 km) for 100 straight days.

Year 3 — The monk must once more run 18.64 miles (30 km) for 100 straight days.

Year 4 — The monk must run 18.64 miles (30 km), this time for 200 straight days.

Year 5 — The monk must again run 18.64 miles (30 km), for 200 straight days. After completing the fifth year of running, the monk must go 9 consecutive days without food, water, or rest. Two monks stand beside him at all times to ensure that he does not fall asleep.

Year 6 — The monk must run 37.28 miles (60 km), per day for 100 straight days.

Year 7 — The monk must run 51.2 miles (84 km), per day for 100 straight days. Yes, you read that correctly - 51.2 miles per day!

Finally, he must run 18.64 miles (30 km), for the final 100 days.

The sheer volume of running is incredible, of course, but there is one final challenge that makes The Kaihogyo unlike any other feat.

Day 101

During the first 100 days of running, the monk can decide it isn't for him and he is allowed to withdraw from the Kaihogyo.

From Day 101 onwards, there is no withdrawal. The monks carry a length of rope and short sword at all times after this point. Once he starts running on Day 101, the monk must either complete the Kaihogyo ... or take his own life.

The Kaihogyo has only been completed 46 times since 1885. Of these, three people have completed the circuit twice, most recently Yūsai Sakai (1926-2013), who first went from 1973 to 1980 and then, after a half-year break, went again, finishing his second round in 1987 at age 60. **This guy should have a running shoe endorsement!!**

Hundreds of other Tendai who attempted the Kaihogyo are only known by their unmarked graves on the hills of Mount Hiei.

CHAPTER 9 REVIEW
LESSON #6 - FINISH

☐ Finishers are rare, which makes them valuable. Be a Rowan and get the job done on time without causing your superior to look over your shoulder.

☐ Our attention span is a little less than that of a goldfish. Focus and committing to finishing a project are vital.

☐ Finish the drill. Make sure you have an ending point for every drill both. Coaches must stand where they can ensure a great finish occurs.

☐ Finish the play. When we implemented Coach Herman's grading system, it made all the difference for us. Whatever sport you coach, find a way to hold them accountable to finish through the line or the whistle.

☐ Focus on your team to finish in crunch time. Soldiers fall to the level of their training. Call what you've trained on for hours and do not out-think yourself worrying about your opponent.

☐ Finishing is not giving in. Results take time. Allow the Law of Compound Interest to work for you and get 1% better each day to finish.

CHAPTER 10

LESSON #7 – PAYDAY

> *"Winning is the most important thing in my life, after breathing. Breathing first, winning next."*
>
> **George Steinbrenner**
> **Former Owner**
> **New York Yankees**

PAYDAY - GETTING WHAT YOU'VE EARNED

It's always tough the first year a new coach comes in to get his program and culture established. This was true my first year in Grapevine. The players didn't resist the changes in schemes or overall way of doing things a new staff always brings in. They did a great job of participating in our summer strength and conditioning and showed up for practice everyday during the season. It was just 'one of those years.'

Our best college prospect, Sam Barry, got injured during the end of the second game. He missed the next game (we started a freshman at quarterback in his place), but returned for our fourth game against a good Arlington Heights team.

We entered the game with an 0-3 record. Having Sam back gave us hope that maybe we could pull the upset, but unfortunately he reinjured himself early in the game. We moved our freshman, Alan Bowman, back down to the junior varsity that week so we didn't have a true backup available. I'm firm believer that your quarterback of the future must be getting reps on the JV. Our philosophy is we will finish the game if our starter gets injured, but if our second-best quarterback is an underclassman, he should be playing and not standing each week.

The game got ugly in a hurry. They had much more team speed than we did and broke one long run after another. In the third quarter, the score was 60-0. We were having zero fun, sir. The final was 60-14 and we had lost Sam for several weeks (it ended up being for the remainder of the year).

We did finish 3-7 and got into the playoffs. Our guys had a great attitude all year and we got better each week. We were bounced 35-21 in the first round by a very good Wichita Falls Rider team.

Now that the season was over, it was time to build our program. The Rider game was on Thursday so we had a team meeting the next day. I have a set routine for our postseason meeting. Our coaching staff thanked the seniors and told them they had laid the foundation for what our program was about to become. We

EVOLUTION – SLOW, CONTINUOUS CHANGE OVER A LONG PERIOD TIME.

REVOLUTION – SUDDEN, RADICAL OR COMPLETE CHANGE.

allowed them to speak to the team and a few of them did. After the seniors spoke the team elected four captains from our leadership council. We formed two lines and 'high-fived' the seniors as they exited the locker room, giving them a standing ovation.

Now it was time to get down to business. I didn't sugarcoat what the next few months would be. In 2014, I arrived in March. Not late, but also not in time to have a 'real' offseason and put them through the ringer. We lifted and ran, but we also started installing the offense and defense to prepare for spring ball that began at the end of April. If I had it to do all over again, I would've found a way to do some type of boot camp. Even if I was the only one who ran it, it would have been something to show them the importance of attention to detail and it's always good to incorporate something new when you arrive to show them changes are about to happen.

There are two basic philosophies coaches use when they go into their first offseason with a struggling program; the first being the evolution method (ease them into it and make sure you don't have too many quit). Or, do what we did. We did what I always do; the revolution method. We tore it down to the studs and hated losing the ones who quit, but we were going to get our 'minds right'. I'm in Grapevine for the long haul and only wanted to line up with guys who 'can't live without it' in 2015 and beyond so we were going to set the standard right then.

PAYDAYS COME AT A COST. YOU CAN'T CHANGE A CULTURE WITHOUT LOSING A FEW GUYS THE FIRST YEAR.

We got after them hard. One coach said on his exit interview, "Randy grinded their corn everyday. It was not a fun place to be."

Standing on the sideline during 2014 wasn't much fun either. On the first official day of offseason, we showed our team a clip against a district opponent from 2014 where four guys could have laid out and made the tackle, but all chose not to. The runner scored from 60 yards out.

I didn't know how good we would be in 2015, but I knew I was going to battle with players who had paid a price to put on the uniform.

In December and January, we wrestled in addition to the normal weightlifting and agility. It was very tough. We have a school wrestling team and coaches who know how to teach the techniques. In February, we began track workouts in addition to our weight program. In the middle of February, we began annual boot camp.

> *"Always trade discomfort now for victory later. Being uncomfortable will always be an ingredient for success."*
>
> **Eddie Pinero**
> **YourWorldWithin**

We did lose some guys. Every three or four days one would come to me and tell me it just wasn't for him. As much as I knew it was part of the process and we had to do this make us tougher, it was gut-wrenching to go through the mass exodus.

Faith believes without seeing. The ones who stay bought in to what we were selling and believed we would be better in 2015.

Fast-forward to football season. We had more confidence after our 'corn grinding' offseason. We were 2-1 when we met Arlington Heights again, this time in Grapevine. They had quite a few of their good players back. They were 2-0 and had won both games easily.

We jumped out to a surprising 14-0 lead in the first quarter. We played great on defense, like we did all year, and held a 14-7 lead at halftime. In the third quarter, we traded touchdowns to make it 21-14 going into the fourth.

Our crowd was into it and they were loud. Heights had the ball and were driving late in the game. They had so much offensive firepower I never felt great about stopping them, although we had done a great job all night. They scored with a minute left on the clock. On their first PAT attempt they had lineman move so it moved them back five yards. Their next kick hit the upright and bounced back. It was pandemonium on our side of the stadium.

We had a big win for our program. It was just a non-district game, but it was big. We just knocked off virtually the same team that could have beaten us 100-0 the year before.

I was almost in tears after the game. I wasn't happy for me, but for the guys who stuck it out. I've been lucky to win some games in my career, but this one is near the top of the list. Not for me at all, but for the guys who stuck it out when some of their friends weren't.

We weren't getting made fun of by the band like the Poteet guys were before 2010, but our guys weren't getting a lot of 'atta boy's' either. The win didn't get us any closer to a gold ball or the playoffs, but it validated a lot of guys who had paid a heavy price when a lot of people didn't believe. It was a win they EARNED from hard work, months before the game was ever played. Our culture was getting established with a big payday.

After the season I was at a clinic and an opposing coach asked me, "What did ya'll do?" He was the head coach of a team who had beaten us in 2014, but we had defeated in 2015. I wasn't sure what he meant so I didn't really know how to answer. He said again, "Coach, I want to know what ya'll did to change those guys over there. The Mustangs were a different team this year." That sure felt proud to have a coach who I respect ask me what we did to change the culture. I told him thank you and that I was lucky to have some guys who didn't mind earning their payday.

CHAMPIONSHIPS ARE SCHEDULED

Leaders must plan for success. Brian Tracy, leadership consultant, says the most successful people in any type of business think about the future most of the time. "They think about where they are going rather than where they have been. They maintain a positive attitude and think about the opportunities of tomorrow rather than focusing on the problems of the past.

> *"The general who wins the battle makes many calculation in his temple before the battle is fought. The general who loses makes but few calculations beforehand."*
>
> **Sun Tzu**

Bill Walsh is credited for developing the concept of scripting the first plays he would call each game. When Walsh was an assistant coach for the Browns, head coach Paul Brown would ask him for the first few plays we would call. Walsh expanded that list to 10 to 12 plays when he was with the San Diego Chargers. The list grew to 20 at Stanford University and finally 25 with the San Francisco 49ers.

Walsh believed: "Your ability to think concisely, your ability to make good judgments is much easier on Thursday night than during the heat of the game. So we prefer to make our decisions related to the game almost clinically, before the game is ever played. Without question you can make more objective decisions during the week as to what you would do in the game than you can spontaneously as the game is being played. To be honest, you're in a state of stress, sometimes you're in a state of desperation and you're asked to make very calculated decisions. It's rarely done in warfare and certainly not in football; so your decisions made during the week are the ones that make sense."

In other words, Walsh says you shouldn't 'wing it' when calling plays. This is true of everything in your program. Spend the time to prepare and get it right.

MEETING WITH YOUR STAFF

Most programs have regularly scheduled meetings. Our practices are structured and fast-paced. We must meet and all be ready before we go to workout, either in season or out of season. In season we meet each day as a staff in the afternoon after our players leave from weights and film (we have morning practices). On the weekends we meet at 8 a.m. on Saturdays and 1:30 p.m. on Sundays. During the offseason we meet at 6:30 a.m. each morning.

I believe there's a right way to meet. We have a big room with a large conference table in the middle and assigned seating when we meet. I sit at the head of one end and our defensive

'AMAT VICTORIA CURAM'

'VICTORY LOVES PREPARATION'

coordinator, Mike Alexander, sits at the other. The offensive staff is on one side of the table and the defensive staff sits on the other side. We don't have cell phones or laptops. Meetings are a time for us to lock in and get on the same page.

PRE-EVENT WALK-THROUGH

We also do walk-throughs as a staff before we do something new. I stole this idea from Chad Morris at SMU. I was told during his first spring on the hilltop his staff did a walk-through at least four times of everything that would happen at one of their practices.

All coaches walked the path the players would take from the locker room to the practice fields. They then went through the entire practice schedule and where each drill would take place. After this they walked through how the players would leave the field back to the locker room. Coach Morris was leaving nothing to chance. I was at the first SMU spring practice and it was very organized. I didn't know at the time about how much preparation the staff had done, but I could definitely tell they were ready to go.

Our staff now does a walk-through anytime we are doing something new. This summer we will walk through the first day of fall camp, for instance.

POST-EVENT FOLLOW-UP

> *"You connect the dots by looking backwards, not forwards."*
>
> **Steve Jobs**

Another great idea when planning for success is to have a post-event meeting. I've mentioned earlier in this book about interviewing college coaches. One of them told me they have post-event meetings for everything. As soon as the last recruit leaves on a recruiting weekend they meet and figure out how they can make it better.

Doing it right then is a great idea. The next year when your event comes up, trying to remember what could have been improved is a tough task. This year, after spring ball was over, the coordinators and I met and went through every aspect of spring ball. We talked about Brian Cain's 'start – stop – continue' process.

What was good that we need to continue? What do we need to stop doing? What do we need to start doing?

DAILY WINS

Winning is a habit. We've all heard this, but we have to make sure we remember it when trying to build a championship culture. Winning also has to be expected. It can't just come through the leader's vision. Winning must happen everyday. We ask our guys what their 'daily win' is for the day. In our game practice meeting we will discuss individual players' daily wins and unit daily win goals.

I'll ask, "Someone tell me what your daily win is today."

"To finish my blocks, sir."

"To make all the correct strength calls."

"All my snaps will be prefect."

After practice I'll ask these same guys if they achieved their daily win.

> *"You win the trophy, you hold it up, you take a picture and you hand it away and get ready for the next one. Monday morning we will have a staff meeting to begin the process for the next season."*
>
> **Lane Kiffin**
> **Offensive Coordinator**
> **Alabama Crimson Tide**

At their annual clinic this year, Coach Morris told a great story about their struggle to instill the concept of winning during his first spring at SMU. He asked their position players what their daily win for the day was and one unit said, "in our stretch lines our helmets are going to be aligned in the straightest line ever known to man."

"We told them we were going to celebrate daily wins," Morris said, "so I high-fived him and said 'great job!'"

Our position coaches will announce what the daily win is for their unit before practice and we will follow up after practice to see if he feels like it was achieved that day.

HOW TO WIN FOOTBALL GAMES

I have made sure this book would be applicable for any coach and truly want all coaches to benefit, but I know my biggest audience will be football coaches, so I'm going to discuss what we think are the main ways football games are won.

To first win a game you first must not lose it. I touched on this in Lesson #5 – Discipline. Every Wednesday we begin our '48-hour countdown' to game time. In my speech to the team on Wednesday I address our 'recipe for payday.'

Statistics show teams that win these categories each week have a higher chance to win the game:

1. Turnover ratio (in the NFL, teams with +1 turnover ratio win 80% of the time)
2. Explosive plays. We categorize an explosive play as +12 rushing and +16 passing.
3. 3rd down conversions
4. QB sacks
5. Penalty yardage
6. Rushing yardage

We track how many of these we win each week and total at the bottom. I go over this with the team the day after the game, during my Wednesday speech and again the following game day morning to re-emphasize.

HOW WE TREAT THEM AFTER A WIN OR LOSS

We handle our team slightly different most of the time after a win or a loss. After a win we praise them, enjoy the film the next day, but then the '24-hour rule' goes into effect. We tell them they have 24 hours to enjoy a win or be down about a defeat.

> *"If you are batting a .1000% you are playing in the little leagues."*
>
> **Warren Buffett**
> **Business Magnate and Investor**

Winning can make a team over-confident. They can start believing what everyone is saying about them and become softer mentally if you're not careful. We're tougher on our team after a win than we are after a loss.

When we do come out on the short end of the stick we teach and correct, but we make sure they know we are sticking by them. They have to know we believe in them.

AT TIMES YOU MUST BE A RISK-TAKER

In 1999, Paducah gave me my first opportunity to be a head coach. We got better as the season progressed and faced the Munday Moguls in Week 8 with a 5-2 record. Back then, only two teams advanced to the playoffs and we had two really good teams in our district; Munday and Aspermont. If we were going to get in the playoffs, we were going to have to beat one of them.

> YOU CANNOT BE AFRAID TO 'STICK YOUR NECK OUT' AND TAKE A CHANCE. PRACTICE YOUR 'SPECIALS' EACH WEEK AND YOUR CONVERSION RATE WILL BE HIGH.

Munday is a traditional power. A good season for them is to not only get in the playoffs, but advance a few rounds. All of their players expect to be playing at Thanksgiving. We had our hands full, but we were at home and riding a five-game winning streak.

The game was a defensive battle. We scored first, but didn't convert the extra point. Munday tied the game right before half, but their extra point was true. At halftime it was a nail-biter, 7-6 Moguls.

We traded punts in the third quarter with neither team able to do much. I was starting to think it might take a turnover and a short field for us to have a chance to pull this one out.

Culture Defeats Strategy

About midway through the fourth quarter we had the ball a little past the 50-yard line, but it was 3rd and 20. Anyone who has ever called plays in football knows the odds of converting 3rd and long are not very good, especially with 20 yards to go. We had one trick up our sleeve so I decided to roll the dice. I called the hitch and pitch. It wouldn't get us a first down, but it might get 10-12 yards and give us a better shot at converting on 4th down.

A hitch route is a six-yard stop pattern. The receiver comes off the ball hard and gets the defensive back to backpedal then puts on the brakes and stops. We saw lots of 'off coverage' in the late '90s so we threw a lot of hitches; just not on 3rd and 20. We had practiced it for a few weeks so I did expect us to execute it ... and we did.

Munday played a soft coverage (Cover 3) that allowed us to complete the hitch. Our quarterback, Pete Cruz, completed it to Steven Dozier who turned and soft-tossed it to Aaron Wederski, who was swinging out of the backfield. The corner never saw Wederski and bit hard to tackle the Dozier. When Aaron caught it he was full stride and going down the sideline. The safety couldn't make the play and Wederski scored. The final was 12-7 Dragons.

This is when I learned first-hand you have to have something up your sleeve. We were a run-based offense like most people at that time. We averaged about 100 yards a game through the air so converting on 3rd and 20 was not going to happen with our best passing play; the bootleg. Heck, we throw it quite a bit more now and if I ask for help on a 3rd and 20 call everyone is going to suddenly get 'lock jaw' because all teams are in deep trouble converting 3rd and long.

If we wouldn't have carried a 'plan B' into the game with us, we may not have won. We advanced all the way to the quarterfinals that season so it was a tremendous way to get our program and my career going. Without the 'hitch and pitch' I don't believe we would've even made the playoffs.

Fast-forward to the playoffs that same season. We won our first-round game, 20-19 over Chico. We were outgained in every statistical category so it was a great win that we could've let slip away.

We would now face the Rotan Yellowhammmers in round two. Head coach Bob Shipley led Rotan to a 9-2 record. His son, Jordan, was a freshman, but a key contributor. Jordan went on to play receiver at the University of Texas and the Cincinnati Bengals. We had our hands full.

They had size and speed. We would be the underdog and would have to play well to have a chance. I figured we needed a couple of more tricks up our sleeve.

I called my mentor, Phil Blue, and asked him if he had anything that we might use to 'steal' a touchdown.

"Granbury has a great swinging gate play they run from the middle of the field after a kickoff return. It's something we have seen on film and we always have to spend time to prepare for it," he told me.

The head coach at Granbury, Biff Peterson, was actually

my old boss from when I was an assistant at Tyler Lee High School. Coach Peterson gave me the rundown on the play and we installed it *that day.*

> **"Do you want to be safe and good, or do you want to take a chance and be great?"**
>
> **Jimmy Johnson**
> **Former Head Coach**
> **Dallas Cowboys**

I don't encourage you to do this. We don't install gadget plays the week of the game anymore, especially ones I am trying to understand by diagramming on the phone in the teacher workroom.

We're more prepared now in our 'specials.' We have 10 for the year and rep three at a time. When we use one in a game we take it out of the rotation and move the next one up. We have a four-minute gadget period in our practice schedule twice a week.

Here's my point — we were outmanned and we needed something to give us a 'momentum shift.' We worked on the swinging gate play all week. We had parents come watch practice and they were probably thinking I was an idiot.

I decided if we won the toss we would receive so we could begin the game with our new play, 'Pirate' (named after the Granbury Pirates).

We won the toss and took the ball. We returned the ball to our hash so we would set up our huddle on our sideline and Rotan would have a tougher time figuring out what was going on.

After we were tackled near the 30-yard line we huddled on our sideline, inside the numbers on the field to be legal. There were ten guys in a two-line huddle facing me. I told them to relax and have fun ... we were about to hit them with something they weren't ready for.

When the whistle blew in for play the ten guys jogged out to the field, but stopped six yards from the ball. They were still in a two-line huddle; six guys on the line of scrimmage and four behind. Once they got set I sent out the last guy, Erik Hinojosa. He jogged past the huddle, not in too big of a hurry as to not draw suspicion. Erik sat over the ball for 1 second (has to do this to be legal) and then 'spun' the ball underhanded to the nearest man in the second line of the huddle, Aaron Wederski (our speed guy).

They weren't ready for this. Our first line went down the field between the hash and the top of the numbers and mowed down all who were now in pursuit. Our second line of guys ran down the bottom of numbers and blocked guys who made it through the first wall of blockers. It was awesome to see all this happen from my vantage point. Coach Peterson told me one or two guys may figure this out right before the ball is snapped so be ready to have to block them from the beginning. None of them sniffed it out, but to be honest my guys wouldn't have either. Who would be thinking about the swinging gate play to open a second-round playoff game? Wederski made it all the way to the six-yard line before their backside corner caught him and pushed him out of bounds.

We had them on their heels after the first play. I wish I could say we scored the next play, but embarrassingly we were so excited we had a hard time getting personnel in for the next play and we got a five-yard penalty! We did score on the drive.

We weren't done with using our specials. Our main running play was the toss sweep so we put in the toss pass that week also. In the second quarter, Wederski (who else) threw a beautiful toss pass to receiver, Eric Richardson and he scored from 30 yards out.

Right before halftime we lined up for a field goal. We had been working a fake field goal since Week 5 or so but hadn't called it. I decided now was the time. We ran 'Idalou' (named after the school who had run it) and it worked perfectly. The holder took the snap and flipped it to the left wing coming behind him. The kicker fakes kicking the ball to help draw attention away from the reverse. In practice we actually have him untie his shoe and kick his shoe through the goal post, it is not only hilarious, but a couple of defenders will watch it instead of the reverse that is happening. I haven't had the guts to go 'full Idalou' in a game, though.

We were up 24-7 at the half, but had only *12 yards of total offense* not generated from a gadget play. I remember telling the coaches (all four of them), "if we don't figure out a way to make some first downs we're going to lose this game." I knew we couldn't keep tricking them. For one reason we were out of trick plays!

We held on and won the game 34-24. After the game, Coach Shipley, one of the real good guys in our profession, talked about our swinging gate play. He asked, "What was that? I was putting on my headphones and heard a loud roar. When I looked up your guy was running down your sideline."

One of my parents came up to me after the game and admitted, "All week I watched us practice that and thought it was stupid. What a great play and way to start the game, coach."

Don't be afraid to have a trick play, or two. Just make sure you rep them in twice a week in a 'specials period' and get good at them. When you execute, your players will believe in them and your success rate will go up even more. Even when they don't work, your opponents will see them on film and have to spend time to prepare to stop them.

> *"Winning isn't everything, but it sure beats anything that comes in second."*
>
> **Bear Bryant**
> **Former Head Football Coach**
> **Alabama Crimson Tide**

PAYDAY

We have to win games to keep our jobs. Coaching is unlike any other profession. We get evaluated once a week (or more if you coach another sport than football) and the media posts our results. The general public can come give their 'two cents' as well.

As much as I want God to 'high-five' me when I meet him

because our program helped build young men into champions of character, if we don't win I will not be allowed to stay. With message boards, Twitter and all the interaction on social media, public opinion has never been easier to express.

I love the concept of 'the process.' I've been told the New England Patriots do not have anything at their complex that mentions all the Super Bowl championships. The assistant coaches do not have their names on their office doors. It isn't about the past or who's coaching what, it's about getting better that day.

Are you getting your desired results? You get what you earn. You must be intentional about creating a championship culture. Take these strategies and put them in place and you will see results. These leadership lessons will not only help your program win more games, but win more student-athletes in the process through relationships.

> **"The man who wants to lead the orchestra must be willing to turn his back on the crowd."**
>
> **Max Lucado**

I have already begun working on a companion book to go along with Culture Defeats Strategy; 'A Weekly Playbook to Culture Defeats Strategy.' It will have more specific strategies to help any coach take his/her program to the next level. The Weekly Playbook will be an in-depth look at our week-to-week system of creating a championship culture that will help any program to grow and flourish.

Thank you for purchasing this book. It was a true honor to talk about some of my former players, teams and my experiences. I believe each player deserves to play for a coach who builds them into a leader, fascinates them and is in a program they 'can't live without'

Make sure you are taking notes along your journey because we all need to write a book.

CHAPTER 10 REVIEW
LESSON #7 - PAYDAY

☐ Payday is earned. Be prepared to have some who are not willing to pay the price.

☐ Championships are scheduled. Meeting everyday is necessary to make sure all coaches are ready to go before each workout. Make sure your meeting time is organized and structured.

☐ Walk-throughs and follow up meetings are both excellent ways to ensure successful events.

☐ Have daily wins and discuss them afterward workout.

☐ Each sport has fundamental ways games are won and lost. Post, track and discuss frequently.

☐ Don't be afraid to take a risk when you are out-manned by an opponent. Make it a calculated risk with preparation and planning.

☐ Take action from the principles and lessons from this book for your programs payday.

ABOUT THE AUTHOR

WHO IS RANDY JACKSON?

> *"For while bodily training is of some value, godliness is of value in every way, as it holds promise for the present life and also for the life to come."*
>
> 1 Timothy 4:8

Knute Rockne, Winston Churchill, Lou Holtz, Bill Parcells were all motivators who would use everything and anything to inspire their team or as in Churchill's case their country to a win. Like them, I have witnessed Coach Jackson use everything and anything to inspire his team at Grapevine. To win means your culture has to have volume and vision that is heard loud and seen clearly. It means there is buy in and people are moved in a direction. It also means that throughout life you will have learned a lesson or two that has a way bigger meaning than just winning a game or two, even a state championship (which would be WAY cool) but culture speaks life and I guess that's where I come in.

My name is John Earle and I serve as Grapevine Football's unofficial team chaplain or spiritual coach. Others in today's politically-correct world would probably call me a character coach, but whatever title you give me I know one thing is true, WE ARE DOING LIFE with the boys and Coach Jackson has allowed me to be a part of this culture because life is what he's all about.

I've been blessed to be around the game of football my whole life, being introduced to it at the age of nine. I can still remember that day as if it were yesterday. It was a cold but sunny January day, 1977 to be exact. I was at my grandfather's place, eating chips and pretzels, and then it happened ... there on the television, the most beautiful setting I have ever seen. Colors were popping. Green, purple, yellow, black and silver ... it was Super Bowl Sunday, the Vikings vs. the Raiders. I fell in love with football that day. At 48 years old, I still have not kicked it to the curb.

From Pop Warner to the NFL, the football locker room has always been viewed in my eyes as an extension of my own family with lessons I believe I have learned at every level that still stick with me today. I've spent many a day in a locker room — five years of Pop Warner, four years in high school, five years in college, five years in the NFL and two years in the CFL (Canadian Football league). I love the camaraderie and togetherness that is found and taught. I played for many teams and coaches, played with many players, and experienced many different types of CULTURES. I have seen and heard them all. From Parcells to Marty Schottenheimer, Coach Jackson's CULTURE ranks up or near the top of them all.

Coach Jackson has spelled out his program values in this book. Although I love them all, the one that hits my heart is what I believe to be our mission statement for Grapevine football — TOUGHNESS. It 's on every piece of workout gear, uniforms, helmets, letterhead and signage.

Toughness is what Coach Jackson and Grapevine football bleed. I remember a conversation early on in my duty as chaplain and Coach Jackson said to me, "I just want our team to be tough and the winning will take care of itself."

Coach has allowed me to 'do life' with our players. My loud style fits right in with the Mustang culture. I love the culture talk he has developed with the team. His culture talk spills over into everyday life with this team.

I'm also the student minister at First Colleyville, a Baptist church in Colleyville Texas. I can tell you first-hand what I see outside the football operations of this culture.

Many a student from 12th all the way down to 8th grade have become a part of my youth group and I see culture first-hand working off the field. Because Coach Jackson has constantly preached to his team "family that plays together stays together," I get to witness this on Wednesday night. I see these ballers literally hanging with each other, they have really grown off the field. Coach Jackson's approach is team, not individualism, but team. I see it at practice, in the locker room, game night, life, team, team, team, that's culture.

LOVE! Its one thing to say it, but another thing to share it, live it and apply it. Coach Jackson has said many times that he loves you. Whether a coach or a player, if you a part of this culture you are going to hear coach say he loves you. There have been many times he has brought me in to talk with a kid who is making bad choices. He has afforded me the opportunities to visit with those in need and it had nothing to do with football ability. It was the culture, the family, the love, and wanting to help a young person right a wrong.

Coach goes hard, y'all!

There isn't a minute that goes by that he isn't coaching

something, from how to address the team, scheming offensive plays, player progress, grades, culture, practice, 1% better every day. I am telling you, coach is 0-60 in a sports car 24/7.

In closing, I would like to say how much I appreciate Coach Jackson giving me the opportunity to be the team's spiritual and character coach. I am allowed to share with the team, dads, and community members each and every Friday at Breakfast of Champions, as well as his annual Mom's 101.

All in all, Coach Jackson has built something special here. I feel he has developed a culture that will not only allow Grapevine to compete and contend for state championships, but create men of character for years to come.

Thanks again for taking the time to read this book. I hope it gave you some new ideas on leadership, culture and program building.

Tough People Win!!!

WHAT'S NEXT?

CULTURE DEFEATS STRATEGY 2 – THE YEARLY PLAYBOOK

The next book in the Culture Defeats Strategy series lays out a yearly calendar of culture and leadership building strategies.

'The Yearly Playbook' takes the foundation of our core values described in this book to another level with a close-up look at how we are intentional throughout the year in our **4-quarter process.**

Visit
CoachRandyJackson.com/Playbook
to learn more!

SPEAKING

WANT RANDY TO COME SPEAK TO YOUR TEAM/ORGANIZATION?

Randy has inspired thousands of coaches and corporate executives around the country to create a culture that takes performance to the next level.

His engaging, interactive presentation provides countless ideas and a tangible plan of action to help you get started!

Visit
CoachRandyJackson.com/Speaking
to book Randy for your next event!

The Jackson Family
Russ, Katie, Shannon and Randy

Made in the USA
Lexington, KY
19 June 2018